Praise for

THE CREATIVE SHIFT

"To succeed—even survive—long term, any institution must creatively change. Andrew Robertson has likely helped more legacy companies make such essential shifts than anyone in recent times. This is an essential book for senior executives and management scholars alike."

—Frederick W. Smith, founder and executive chairman, FedEx Corporation

"Here is your chance to learn from one of the most impressive and consistently creative minds I have had the pleasure to work with in my career. Every company needs to harness creativity, and *The Creative Shift* gives you the insight and practices of an industry icon who has embedded himself in some of the world's great companies, harnessing creativity to solve the most pressing market challenges when they were needed most."   —John Stankey, chairman and CEO, AT&T Inc.

"There is a belief that operators and builders can't coexist. In *The Creative Shift*, Robertson dispels that notion. He describes ways that leaders can ingrain a mindset, a process for creativity and a passion for growth. Importantly, he shows that these disciplines can work in every company: old and young; big and small. This book drips with credibility, written by one of my favorite partners—a leader who delivers groundbreaking results for clients time and again."

—Jeff Immelt, former CEO, General Electric

"Robertson has been a creative force for over forty years, and he has been a wildly successful leader because he understands that the inevitable shifts in the marketplace, and among consumers, require constant innovation, curiosity, and creativity. As someone who has both started new businesses and reinvented legacy businesses, from MTV to AOL and iHeartMedia, I know this book will be an invaluable resource for every leader, marketer, and innovator who wants their teams and organizations to understand—and take advantage of—these shifts."

—Bob Pittman, chairman and CEO,
iHeartMedia, Inc.

"There are books that present readers with the latest trends and those that ground readers in practical advice. This book does both. I loved the focus Robertson brings to the continued need to foster and unleash creativity in any organization—no matter the size."

—Carla Hassan, chief marketing officer,
JPMorgan Chase

"BBDO chairman Andrew Robertson argues the fundamentals of good business—excellence, discipline, predictability—are all too often at odds with an organization's most underleveraged asset: human creativity. In *The Creative Shift*, he tells snackable stories, culled from decades of award-winning collaborations, that demonstrate how leaders can enable teams to realize their true potential."

—Richard Dickson, CEO, Gap Inc.

"In this book, Robertson reaffirms a timeless principle by which he has lived all his life. Creativity is a differentiator and a tangible accelerator for growth. In no time has this become more essential than in the age of generative AI. The good news? Your people have the creativity! Robertson shows us how to uncover and leverage it."

—Antonio Lucio, EVP and chief marketing
and corporate affairs officer, HP Inc.

THE
CREATIVE
SHIFT

THE CREATIVE SHIFT

HOW TO POWER UP
YOUR ORGANIZATION
BY MAKING SPACE
FOR NEW IDEAS

ANDREW ROBERTSON

BASIC
VENTURE

New York

Basic Venture
Hachette Book Group
1290 Avenue of the Americas, New York, NY 10104
www.basic-venture.com

Printed in the United States of America

First Edition: September 2025

Published by Basic Venture, an imprint of Hachette Book Group, Inc. The Basic Venture name and logo is a registered trademark of the Hachette Book Group.

The Hachette Speakers Bureau provides a wide range of authors for speaking events. To find out more, go to www.hachettespeakersbureau.com or email HachetteSpeakers@hbgusa.com.

Basic Venture books may be purchased in bulk for business, educational, or promotional use. For more information, please contact your local bookseller or the Hachette Book Group Special Markets Department at special.markets@hbgusa.com.

The publisher is not responsible for websites (or their content) that are not owned by the publisher.

Print book interior design by Bart Dawson.

Library of Congress Control Number: 2025931852

ISBNs: 9781541705241 (hardcover), 9781541705265 (ebook)

LSC-C

Printing 1, 2025

To my dad

CONTENTS

INTRODUCTION

When I think about all I've learned about business and creativity after a forty-plus-year career in advertising, I'm still amazed at how I basically fell into the field at 2:30 in the morning at a nightclub in Maidenhead just outside London.

I was a college student, living with my parents, and had a part-time job selling life insurance. I used to make a hundred cold calls on a Monday night; from those I would get ten appointments, which in turn would lead to three sales and about $500 in commission—enough to fund a rather louche lifestyle when you're living at home and borrowing your mother's car.

The appointments were always in the evening, and when I finished I would make my way to the Valbonne nightclub, where I would go disco dancing in my high-waisted pleated trousers and well-ironed shirt until it closed at 2 a.m. Sometimes this was followed by a few rounds of backgammon at the Royal Berkshire Hotel. I would go home, sleep for a few hours, and then take the train to London in the morning for lectures.

Rinse. Repeat.

One morning my father surprised me by saying matter-of-factly over breakfast, "You may not have thought about this yet, but you know this can't go on."

I was taken aback. "What do you mean?" I asked.

He responded, "We're okay with supporting you while you do your degree, but the day you graduate you need to get your own place or else pay us rent. And you need to get your own car or start paying your mother for using hers."

I was mortified. It suddenly dawned on me that my carefree lifestyle was going to collapse.

In the early hours of the following morning, as they were putting the chairs on the tables at the Valbonne and starting to turn up the lights, I looked around and saw a guy I recognized. I didn't know him very well, but I did know he was at the Valbonne almost as often as I was, and also that he had an Alfa Romeo. So I turned to him and said, "What do you do for a living?"

He said, "I'm an account director at an advertising agency."

And I said to him, "I'm going to do that, then."

They say it's important to have a purpose in life. Mine was to get an Alfa Romeo.

It wasn't deep. But it was clear. And I'm grateful that it serendipitously led me to a wonderful career that included, for twenty years, being CEO of the BBDO Worldwide advertising agency. A career that has allowed me to work very closely with, and see deep inside, a wide array of businesses in every category, from media to manufacturing to retail to entertainment to insurance to consumer goods to airlines and beyond.

And it has enabled me to help organizations develop ways to achieve what I call the Creative Shift: a deliberate and strategic choice to design the conditions that will unleash creativity when an organization needs it the most.

As varied as the businesses we work with are, they have one thing in common: They all encounter times when they need to find completely new creative solutions to either new or old problems. Examples: A new competitor has entered the scene and is grabbing market share. Sales for a long-reliable profit source have begun flagging. New environmental rules demand new manufacturing methods. A new technology is starting to endanger a company's very reason for being.

It's inevitable: A shift in the market will demand a shift in products, services, and messaging.

And the pace of these shifts is accelerating. I've seen it over time in my own industry. After I decided to go into advertising on that fateful night at the Valbonne, I picked a topic for my senior economics dissertation that would enable me to interview senior people in advertising agencies as "research" that I could use to get my foot in the door. I chose something I considered to be especially cutting-edge:

the introduction of color magazines to Sunday print newspapers. Sounds rather old-fashioned, now that most newspaper publishing is online.

For decades, print ads, along with TV and radio commercials and billboards, were reliably the best way for companies to spread their message. During my tenure at BBDO Worldwide, though, my industry has been transformed by three seismic and technologically driven changes: the spread of the internet; the introduction of the smartphone; and, most recently, the rise of generative AI. We have repeatedly had to rethink our ways of working to adjust to emerging realities. And it's the same for just about every other industry out there.

I've seen firsthand just how hard it is for companies to inject creativity into their operations—even when their leaders know and proclaim how necessary it is. The reason? Because creativity is scary and uncertain, and it requires letting go of the tried-and-true.

This book is for every leader, manager, and entrepreneur who needs to rally a team or organization to think big when everyone's instincts scream "hide." What we at BBDO have developed through trial and error is a way of keeping the flame of creativity burning brightly under suffocating pressure—which happens to be when you most urgently need creative problem-solving.

Making a Creative Shift can be especially challenging for a company that thrives precisely because of its focus on precision and operational excellence. Challenging but not impossible. The airline industry offers a perfect example of a company that was able to do it successfully.

With a culture built around safety and timeliness, Delta Airlines moved into a more creative space as it sought to make the travel experience more enjoyable and rewarding for its passengers by eliminating pain points and reducing stress.

They did their research in a creative way. Using activity trackers to monitor volunteer passengers' heart rates, they were able to identify the moments of greatest stress throughout the entire travel process—from the night before, through the journey to and through the airport, to the flight itself, to picking up checked bags, to getting a cab to a hotel, and to checking in.[1]

Turns out that flying in a metal tube at 35,000 feet isn't the most stressful part of the journey, judging by heart rates. Instead, anxiety surged at multiple moments before takeoff and after landing. Before: What time should I leave for the airport? Will there be a big line at the check-in desk? Will there be delays? I wonder if my bags made it onto the plane. After: Will my bag be at the carousel? Will I be able to get a cab? Off the tarmac, pulses were pounding.

Then Delta got really creative, asking, "What can we do for our passengers to reduce this stress, when we can't control the weather, the traffic, or the airport itself?"

The shift lay in connecting travelers, through the Delta app, to information that the airline already had.

As a major airline, Delta already had excellent weather and traffic data. Why not use it by connecting it to some mapping software and a rideshare service so that the airline could ping you the night before your trip with a message? On the order of: We are expecting rain tomorrow so you should allow extra time to get to the airport. We recommend you leave your house at 10 a.m. if you're planning to drive yourself and park, or 10:30 a.m. if you're getting a ride. Would you like us to book you a Lyft? You can pay for it with 500 SkyMiles.

And the app could notify passengers about when their checked bags were on the plane, because Delta obviously already had that information from the barcodes on the luggage tags. All it had to do was give it to the passengers. The company even found that telling someone that a checked bag had *not* made it onto the plane reduced stress versus not knowing one way or the other.

All these measures helped to reduce the anxiety levels of passengers—a brilliant example of looking at a problem through a creative lens while keeping the planes in the air and on time.

Creativity demands divergent thinking, where you open yourself up to as many ideas as you can. Running a successful business day to day, though, often depends on following a well-optimized and proven process, without the chaos and confusion caused by someone's new ideas. Everyone knows when they need new ideas. It's harder to know how to get them while holding on to what's working.

Because business-as-usual inherently conflicts with creativity, leaders must visibly signal to their teams (and to themselves) when a different mode is needed. Since many of the routines required for hitting goals, deadlines, and key performance indicators can, and should, be structured and disciplined, they are intrinsically incompatible with the sense of play required for creativity, and effective organizations strive to separate them. They develop systems and practices for turning the creative function on and off like a faucet.

The company I led has a long history of creativity. It was named as a much-feared competitor to the ad agency featured in the AMC series *Mad Men*. BBDO nearly dealt a death blow to the fictional Sterling Cooper when it grabbed the lucrative Lucky Strike account away from them.

BBDO, short for Batten, Barton, Durstine, and Osborn, had already been in business for decades when it posed this threat to Sterling Cooper. (In real life, on his radio show in 1948, the comedian Jack Benny unsuccessfully tries to reach one of the founders of the firm, a sponsor of the show, as his wife, Mary Livingstone, jokes that the full name "sounds like a trunk falling downstairs.")

The firm started in 1928 when the George Batten advertising company (formed in 1891) merged with the Barton, Durstine, and Osborn firm. The companies—which had been wary competitors—both happened to have offices in the same building on Madison Avenue.

After the merger, in short order, the unwieldy name became a quartet of initials. BBDO had such a nice ring to it—and the agency's work quickly became so admired—that we're still known by the initials of our long-dead founders nearly a century later.

In the 1930s, Alex Osborn, the non-rhyming "O" in BBDO, began working on the concept of "organized ideation," which evolved into something he called "brainstorming." In the 1940s he held hundreds of brainstorming sessions a year at BBDO. Through his writings, Osborn popularized the concept of brainstorming to the point that it became, and remains, a household word.

Brainstorming has been a part of BBDO's success ever since.

When I became CEO of BBDO Worldwide in 2004, though, I felt that we needed to update and codify the principles of brainstorming that Alex Osborn had pioneered. And so the WorkOut—a highly structured process that takes brainstorming to a whole new level—was born.

Some academics have pooh-poohed the idea of brainstorming. They assert that the best creative ideas arise from individuals working alone. But most of these critics are judging the process as it usually occurs, without the key practices that we at BBDO have put in place.

Yes, if you put ten or twelve people around a conference table and say, "How can we be more creative?" then the extroverts and the blowhards will probably dominate the conversation; the introverts will be afraid or unwilling to speak; and groupthink and snap negative judgments will most likely poison the proceedings.

But by adopting our proven idea-generating principles, you can avoid these perils. The chapters that follow will show you how to:

+ Zero in on defining the problem you're actually try-ing to solve (it's trickier than you might think).
+ Create an environment where *all* people—even the finance managers and the lawyers and the factory workers—are able to be creative. Because they are.
+ Bring people together from widely different back-grounds to work on a creative challenge.
+ Create a separate space where people can be silly, stupid, and wrong. A lot. Because that's what you need to do to find the brilliant ideas that need to be unearthed.
+ Suspend all negative judgment during the idea-generation phase (*very* hard to do without practice and structure).

You will also discover how:

+ Thinking and playing like a toddler can release un-tapped creativity.
+ Removing the conference table from a meeting room is one of the simplest ways you can spark group cre-ativity. (Also, get rid of the whiteboard.)
+ Asking for the contents of someone's "secret drawer" can yield surprising and useful ideas.

Not only will I show you how to make the best of your idea-generating sessions, I'll also give you advice on cre-ating a culture, and encouraging regular habits, that will make your organization's creative efforts exponentially more fruitful.

BBDO's work is about much more than advertising campaigns. Our creative principles—whether they've involved WorkOuts or not—have directly or indirectly helped companies reimagine themselves and even affected societal mores. They aided General Electric in coming up with vastly more fuel-efficient jet engines. They led to Procter & Gamble ad campaigns that helped challenge sexist attitudes around menstruation and housework in India. And they played a role in helping Mattel reinvent and revive an iconic blonde doll whose relevance, and sales, were flagging (eventually leading to a blockbuster 2023 movie).

Depending on your industry, the time you need to spend on a Creative Shift will vary. An ad agency like ours needs to do it constantly. A company that, say, manufactures automotive parts will need to exercise its creative muscle much less frequently. But that doesn't mean doing so is any less important.

Whatever the size or type of your business—and whether you're a leader, manager, employee, or entrepreneur—you can use the ideas in this book to help make the Creative Shift. It's a proven way to nurture creative contributions—new products, new services, new solutions—without losing the ability to keep the rest of the business alive and well.

1

WHY THE CREATIVE SHIFT WORKS

*C*reativity is good.

    Organizations need creative people.

Leaders must nurture new ideas.

Who would disagree with these statements?

Almost no one.

Yet many leaders who say they know the value of creativity act as if it's the last thing they want factored into their day-to-day operations.

Few are happy to stub their toe on a new idea. Even at BBDO, where creativity is our bread and butter, it can be hard. How do you know when to begin, and, more importantly, when to stop? When someone suggests an idea with the potential to stall forward motion, people visibly tighten up. Can't we just get on with this, even if the current approach isn't *perfect?*

Just because people like an idea doesn't mean they're instantly going to fall in love with it or act on it. That's because they can often see things in it that are frightening. Or complicated and expensive. And that will cloud their view of it.

These people have failed to fully grasp what can seem like a paradox: Creativity is good, except when it isn't. A lot of the time when you're running a business, the very kinds of ideas and processes that make you successful are going to impede your ability to be creative. The key to maximizing creativity is to understand that nurturing it requires the conscious development and application of a whole different set of rules.

My definition of creativity as it applies to advertising is that it is the magical ability to capture and hold the attention of an audience while giving them a demonstration, some information, or an experience that changes the way they think, the way they feel, and the way they behave.

I define creativity more broadly as finding completely new solutions to either new or old challenges. And the word "completely" matters.

MORE CREATIVITY, BETTER OUTCOMES

Everyone agrees that organizational creativity is important, but does it actually lead to better business results? According to a study by the consulting firm McKinsey, it definitely does.

Much better.

McKinsey used the number and type of Cannes Lions Awards (given to brands and companies for advertising creativity) as a proxy for the creativity of the companies themselves.[1] From there McKinsey came up with something called an Award Creativity Score.

McKinsey found that the brands whose ads received the most awards during a five-year period showed significantly better financial performance—including revenue growth and return to shareholders—than those that received fewer awards. Companies with lower scores, on the other hand, "were far less likely to post above-average financial results."

McKinsey identified several key practices that the most creative leaders embrace:

They weave creativity into the fabric of the company. The senior executives at the most creative companies don't just set creativity as a goal for the company (i.e., everyone else), but see themselves as personally responsible for nurturing it. And they model their behavior accordingly. They make creativity and innovation a topic of conversation in board meetings more than their peers do. And they prioritize and commit the necessary investment to those things.

They are fanatically devoted to customers. Most companies claim to be focused on their customers. Who wouldn't? The key word here is "fanatically." The most creative companies go way beyond traditional research methodologies, such as focus groups and surveys, and use advanced analytics, along with ethnographic and behavioral analysis, to gain a comprehensive and detailed understanding of their customers. Of particular importance, they regularly observe customers in their own world as a way to form a clearer picture of the problems they face and thus to identify how the company can help them.

They are much faster at executing ideas—and measuring the results—than their less creative counterparts. Speed is a competitive advantage. But it can't be an excuse for a lack of rigor and accountability. The best companies define specific deliverables, not vague goals, and make clear who is responsible for what, and when.

I have seen inside some of the most operationally excellent and financially driven companies in the world, including AT&T, FedEx, General Electric, and Visa. I believe that these companies are able to achieve disproportionate success precisely because of the way they are able to complement these capabilities with the Creative Shift.

If creativity demonstrably leads to better results, then why do so many leaders shy away from it? Because it has a cost. Every new idea represents a risk. If time and money weren't obstacles, businesses would try every possibility until one prevailed. The constraints on creative exploration and experimentation are real.

Doing things the way you've always done them, by contrast, seems safe and predictable—especially when it's been working. But that, too, comes with a cost. It can leave you flat-footed when a nimbler competitor enters the market with a new technology or just a new way of doing the same things you've already been doing. It can cause a great idea to stay hidden in a folder, only to appear fully realized in some other company's product or service. It can even cause what you do to slowly become obsolete.

And yet, the more the ground shifts beneath people's feet, the more they crave certainty. It's a very human response to instability.

Rapid changes in business and society at large have become overwhelming—whatever the industry. External business threats, technological disruption, supply chain issues, media fragmentation, political instability—these are running up against a rising tide of disaffection and burnout among employees. Any of these challenges alone would be enough to keep an executive awake at night. But the combination of internal and external chaos makes for a leadership and management powder keg.

Entrepreneurs, who often need creativity the most, aren't immune to instability, uncertainty, or rapid change either. Living in volatile and unpredictable times inhibits decision-making. Try figuring out how to pivot your new app when that expected round of venture capital funding dries up. If you don't keep your head screwed on tight, you'll run out of ideas before you can taxi to the runway, let alone reach the end of it. When making payroll every month remains an open question, you can't help but push away the ideas you need to reach the next level.

Some psychologists, along with business experts and government officials (including—famously—former Defense Secretary Donald Rumsfeld), have said that to meet new challenges, we must prepare to face "known knowns," "known unknowns," and, most perplexing of all, *"unknown unknowns."*[2]

Known knowns are the easiest kinds of problems to handle, because you clearly understand the problem and what it will take to solve it. With known unknowns, your knowledge of the problem may be mistaken, or only partial and imperfect, but at least you know the kind of risk you're taking when you tackle it. But the unknown unknowns are so out of left field that you didn't even know they were coming (a worldwide pandemic would be an example).

You're going to need creativity for new opportunities and growth. But you're also going to need it to deal with the unknown unknowns when they happen—and they will.

All those known knowns, known unknowns, and especially unknown unknowns breed anxiety. And that anxiety is highly transmissible. Part of my job as a leader is to be an insulator, not a lightning rod. I need to shield my people from as much outside anxiety as I can, so they can do what they need to do and focus on that—because transmitting and sharing all the pressure of multiple unknowns will stifle their ability to be creative.

You only beat the competition to the punch by exploring possibilities more efficiently than they can. This means strategically directing your creative output.

"THERE IS NO MAGIC, ONLY PREPARATION"

Some might find it off-putting to see the words "creativity" and "efficiency" in the same sentence. People don't want to feel like they're on some kind of creative assembly line, after all. What am I trying to do: Take all the magic out of the creative process?

Not at all. The efficiency comes when you're actually setting up the structures, processes, and deadlines that enable creativity to flourish. That's what we've done with our BBDO WorkOuts. Within this highly efficient framework, you see the ideas start to flow and the magic start to happen. Without it, great ideas might never emerge at all.

When BBDO was planning to use the magician David Blaine in a 2007 Mountain Dew soda commercial, he came by the New York agency to discuss it. Standing outside the office of my chief creative officer, David Lubars, with various assistants, art directors, and copywriters nearby, Blaine suddenly levitated about four inches off the floor. Everyone was suitably awestruck.

Afterward, I said to him, "C'mon, David, you've gotta tell me: What's the magic?" And he looked me squarely in the eye and said, "There is no magic, only preparation."

Despite what he said, it *was* a kind of magic. And so is creative thinking. The processes we use at BBDO to make it happen are not magical, but they do set up the conditions for the magic to happen. If you're focused on operational efficiency most of the time, you need to make an intentional and counterintuitive effort to achieve the Creative Shift.

Consider the operationally exacting routines at FedEx. Between the hours of 9 and 10 p.m., more than 6,000 people show up for work at the company's Memphis hub.[3]

Between 10:30 p.m. and 1:15 a.m., 150 FedEx planes land in Memphis, and employees proceed to unload and re-sort 1.5 million packages. Then those same planes are reloaded and take off again to deliver their newly loaded packages.

Now, you are not going to want to get creative at a time and place like this, because this is a fine-tuned operation that runs with the utmost efficiency and precision. But FedEx can and does carve out spaces to be amazingly creative whenever it needs to make a major directional shift.

Companies like FedEx know they must apply the same level of rigor, focus, and drive to their creative efforts as they expend on their operational demands—even though the two can seem at odds with one another.

Operational excellence often requires conformity and process compliance, which are totally justifiable characteristics built into most organizational systems. This is exactly why you must consciously create a space where these qualities are *not* what matters.

And it's not an either/or. You're going to need both. In other words, it is critical to conduct business as usual while creating a time, a space, and a methodology to pursue business that's anything *but* usual.

This dissonance between creativity and control crops up frequently in my interactions with other business leaders. It's critical to strike a balance between operation and exploration. Establish a place, time, context, and approach for creativity. And see new ideas bloom.

WHAT CAN WE LEARN FROM RESTAURANTS?

I spend a lot of time in restaurants. I'm fascinated by the way they work—for example, when the creativity of the best chefs meshes with the perfectly repeated execution of the best line cooks.

I follow the New York restaurateur Keith McNally on Instagram. He's the owner of Balthazar and a number of other New York restaurants that have sustained success over decades in what is a highly faddish business.

I follow him because he is provocative and funny and also informative, as when he publishes the previous day's report from the maître d'. On one Saturday over the holidays in 2023—and this is mind-blowing—Balthazar served 1,001 guests at brunch: "To my count we sat 117 guests in the first 15 minutes," the maître d' reported.[4] "It was non-stop right from when we opened."

Extraordinary care went into the design of the Balthazar space itself. McNally has described it as a film set in which all of the diners are cast members. And the development of the menu was highly creative. The amazing members of the restaurant staff make the experience of being there seem theatrical and magical. In addition, the operational brilliance of the kitchen is second to none.

Will Guidara distinguishes between what he calls "corporate smart" and "restaurant smart"—and the inevitable tension between the two—in his book *Unreasonable Hospitality*.[5] Guidara is a renowned restaurateur and former general manager of the much-awarded restaurant Eleven Madison

Park in New York (it was named the "World's Best Restaurant" in 2017). He is committed to operational excellence. In a low-margin business like restaurants, where the chances of going out of business are high, you need to keep an eagle eye on food costs, hire the best people, stay on top of scheduling and payroll, make sure you're following city food regulations, and so on.

But Guidara knows that even if you are running on all cylinders operationally, diners will never have a truly memorable experience unless a restaurant demonstrates above-and-beyond hospitality. And that requires creativity.

"In restaurant-smart companies, members of the team have more autonomy and creative latitude," Guidara writes. "Corporate-smart companies, on the other hand, have all the back-end systems and controls in areas like accounting, purchasing, and human resources that are needed to make them great businesses, and they're often more profitable as a result. But systems are, by definition, controls—and the more control you take away from the people on the ground, the less creative they can be, and guests can feel that."

Corporate smart doesn't have to stamp out creativity, but it will if it is allowed to fill up every nook and cranny of a business. Customers can tell when they're perceived by staff and management as little more than a data point in a transaction. And they don't like it. As Guidara recounts, "Former navy captain David Marquet says that in too many organizations, the people at the top have all the authority and none of the information, while the people on the front line have all the information and none of the authority." That's how corporate-smart places become "restaurant-dumb," as Guidara puts it.

To strike a balance between control and creativity, Guidara follows something he calls the rule of 95/5: "Manage 95 percent of your business down to the penny; spend the last 5 percent 'foolishly,'" on unreasonably creative ideas meant to make your customers happy. And hopefully to give them an experience they'll never forget. "Because that last 5 percent has an outsize impact on the guest experience, it's some of the smartest money you'll ever spend," he says.

Guidara had followed the 95/5 rule earlier in his career when he was charged with designing a gelato cart for the Museum of Modern Art's Sculpture Garden. Using his connections and operational savvy, he managed to secure some world-class gelato for the cart at an unusually low price. And then he became obsessed with designing the best possible plastic spoon for that gelato—a spoon that would be worthy of occupying the same space as artwork by Henri Matisse, Pablo Picasso, and Henry Moore.

These paddle-shaped spoons were "extraordinarily well designed and completely unique," he writes. "They were also preposterously, heartbreakingly expensive." Were they worth it? Absolutely. He felt validated when he saw a group of visiting museum curators admiring the spoons while on an ice cream break.

Guidara applied the 95/5 principle at Eleven Madison Park with what he called his Dreamweavers program.[6] He gave his people time and agency to dream up personalized dining experiences for diners beforehand—for example, by Googling their names and looking at their public social media accounts. Hosts and waiters were also encouraged to come up with ideas *during* dinner based on things they had heard or overheard during the meal.

And Guidara hired a kind of artistic director and extra staff to transform people's creative ideas into reality. It was this creative space—separate from the restaurant's operational excellence—that led to original, even legendary dining experiences for customers.

And so it was that one out-of-town visitor, who said he had neglected to buy his daughter a stuffed animal, received a teddy bear expertly made out of kitchen towels as a parting gift. And at much greater cost (but still worth it), the restaurant turned a private dining room into a facsimile of a beach, complete with sand and kiddie pool, to console a couple whose flight to a sunny vacation destination had been canceled. Those are just two examples out of many.

How many restaurants have their own production studios? Not a lot. Yes, the Dreamweavers program was elaborate and expensive. (But not always. Sometimes it involved some very fast errand-running, such as having someone rush out to buy ten 100 Grand candy bars to give to a banker who had just joked that he would have preferred a million dollars to the after-dinner drink he was offered.) Many of those diners will be talking about the uniquely personal experience they had at Eleven Madison Park to the end of their days.

WHAT DOESN'T WORK

Guidara is something of a rarity. Too often, leaders recognize that they need an injection of creativity, but then take various well-intentioned approaches to generating new ideas that end up failing to move the needle. Here are examples of the kinds of things they say they want to do, and what actually ends up happening.

"We are not a creative company. We need to become one."
The problem with a directive like this is that there is often a gaping hole between what these leaders claim they value and what they actually do value—between what they say they want from their people and the behavior they actually reward.

For example, one popular mantra, in the name of creativity, is to tell everyone to move fast and break things. A few companies (Meta comes to mind) actually do reward this type of behavior in some cases, and are set up to do so. But do you really want people at companies like Ford or Pfizer or GE to be going around breaking things? I don't think so.

Here's another example: Learn from your mistakes. Boeing did not say to the people whose actions caused a door panel to blow out of an Alaska Airlines plane in midair in early 2024: "That's okay! Just learn from what happened so you don't do it again."

Or how about this one: Ask for forgiveness, not permission. "Sorry I didn't ask you in advance whether I could buy that cheaper part for the assembly line, boss, and that it caused all those major slowdowns. I thought it was a great money-saving idea at the time."

In reality, many companies need to operate much of the time with compliance, consistency, and accuracy in mind. It's only when creativity is called for that they should make a total shift into a different realm.

"We should give this problem to our most creative in-house experts to solve."
Yes, of course you need experts to weigh in on creative challenges. But in order to be truly creative, you should also involve people who know little to nothing about the problem at hand. Experts, with their vast knowledge and experience, are prone to making assumptions that they don't even know they're making. People who know nothing are less afraid to ask the supposedly silly and ignorant questions—the questions that lay bare the misguided assumptions.

This misguided idea about experts makes an assumption in itself: that some people are creative and others are not. In fact, *all* people have the capacity to be creative. They just need to be placed in an environment that unlocks creativity. And when people from a variety of unlike backgrounds get together to generate ideas, the result is incredibly powerful— much more so than if only the experts met.

"We can create a separate unit that develops creative ideas."
I've seen companies set aside resources for so-called skunkworks projects, where a group of brilliant people— often hired from outside—is charged with coming up with

brilliant new ideas. And some of these ideas are indeed incredibly creative. The problem is that even if the transplant works, the body then rejects the organ.

Two major obstacles often get in the way of this approach: One is that once these skunkworks ideas see the light of day, they prove to be impractical and unrealistic. Another is that the ideas tend to meet with immense skepticism within the company. Why? Because the rest of the organization hasn't been involved in the process from the start.

"We'll use focus groups to figure out one great creative solution, and develop it brilliantly from there."

This is an especially dangerous myth. And because so many people believe it, a lot of bad ideas that never should have seen the light of day meet with public mockery, criticism, or indifference. In fact, I've found that only about one in ten ideas is any good. As I'll show later, before you get to a really good and original idea, you need to generate lots and lots of bad ideas. You want leaders and managers to create an environment where it's not just okay to come up with an abundance of "silly" and "crazy" thoughts—it's compulsory.

CREATIVITY VS. INCREMENTAL IMPROVEMENT

In the face of uncertainty, too many leaders respond with incrementality rather than true originality. They make improvements on existing ideas rather than coming up with totally new ones.

And when they introduce one of these improvements, they herald it as an "innovation," which is one of those words that has become so overused that its original meaning has become hopelessly muddied. These days, most people use the word when they are merely improving something. And that is not the essence of creativity.

Another way of thinking about it is this: With "innovation," as it's often defined, the gain is measured in percentages. Creativity, by contrast, is measured in orders of magnitude.

I'll give you a small example of that. My wife and I were leaving a restaurant after dinner in New York one night, and there was a homeless man standing on the sidewalk. He said, "I've done three tours of Afghanistan and I'm homeless, but I'm not bitter." I could appreciate that, and reached into my pocket to see if I had five dollars to give him.

At that point the man turned to my wife and said, "Do you know what the best thing about sleeping with a homeless guy is?" We were both taken aback and ready to rush off immediately, when he said, "After we're done, you can drop me off anywhere." We both burst out laughing. I had to hand it to him, and indeed I handed him all the cash I had. In short, he got exponentially more than I was originally going to give him because of that very creative approach to panhandling.

One executive who knows how to encourage true creativity is James Thompson, a former marketing executive at Unilever, Avon, Diageo, and Heineken. James always gets excited by things that are genuinely new and different. A campaign we worked on with him for the Jamaican beer Red Stripe (then owned by Diageo) is a quintessential example of that.

As James well knows, one of the toughest challenges in beer advertising is brand recognition. Most beer ads look pretty much the same. They seem almost required to show people in social situations drinking and laughing.

Our Red Stripe commercials took an entirely different approach. We created a brand ambassador who was dressed like a bottle of Red Stripe beer, complete with a red sash. The ambassador makes cheerful and outlandish pronouncements, such as, "When ugly people stand next to a bottle of Red Stripe they look beautiful!" And, "A good way to meet people is to wear a Red Stripe sash. But a *great* way of meeting people is to wear *nothing* but a Red Stripe sash!" And, "Red Stripe beer makes a lousy fabric softener. Because it is *not* a fabric softener!"

The commercials conclude with the tagline "Hooray Beer!" Now, those two words might not seem especially clever, but in fact they were. They succeeded in getting quite a few people to say "Hooray Beer!" instead of "Cheers!" when they clinked bottles with their friends.

James was able to see how this seemingly bizarre idea was a big creative leap, because it accomplished three things and three things only. One: It made loud and clear that this was a Red Stripe commercial. Two: It made people laugh, and if you make people laugh they're generally going to like you. And three: It included something inside the advertising that was able to live outside the advertising, the tagline "Hooray Beer!"

Brilliant.

James knows the difference between the business world's increasingly watered-down definition of innovation and a true creative leap.

"The problem with innovation is that people now have innovation departments," James said recently.[7] He has set up innovation units himself, and they do serve a purpose, such as being at the forefront of adding flavors, sizes, colors, and ingredients to a product. But what tends to happen is that they reward predictability, continuity, and repeatability rather than true creative leaps, and "anything that's predictable doesn't require creativity," he said.

If anything, innovation departments have become a victim of their own success, with units tending to set annual goals that can be linked to financial targets, rather than five or ten goals that might or might not work out.

People who work in innovation departments also tend to like market research and trend reports, James added. But, he warned, "if you see something in a trend report, it's already too late. It's almost like, when you see what's in the trend report, you should do the exact opposite. Market research is fantastic if you want to innovate. It's not great if you want a breakthrough."

When a soda company comes up with a brand new flavor, that's an improvement. When the Red Bull company came up with a new drink that combined a lot of caffeine with a flavor that was unlike anything anybody had tasted before, put it in a small can, and priced it at a monstrous premium, it made a genuine creative leap.

When a company adds new ingredients or scents to its cleaning products, that's an improvement. But when Procter & Gamble introduced the Swiffer, that was the result of deeply creative thinking.

When Apple adds features and upgrades to its iPhone, those are improvements. The iPhone itself was one of the greatest creations of all time.

INTRODUCING THE IPHONE

When Steve Jobs took the stage at Macworld in 2007, he wasn't exaggerating when he said he was about to announce a revolutionary new device.[8] It was, he said, "an iPod, a phone, and an internet communicator . . . are you getting it? These are not three separate devices. This is one device, and we are calling it iPhone."

Not only that, but this device would come *without* a physical keyboard.

You could sense the confusion in the audience. Did that mean you would need to carry a mouse around with you at all times? Or (ugh) a stylus? No, Jobs reassured them.

Instead, "we're gonna use a pointing device that we're all born with": our ten fingers, Jobs said. Thanks to a new technology called Multitouch, people would be able to summon their keyboard on demand, and then send it back into the ether to receive the full visual benefit of their phone screen.

It was a stunning Creative Shift that hardly anyone had seen coming, thanks to Jobs's penchant for secrecy. People around the world were awed.

One huge beneficiary of the iPhone was our client AT&T, which was able to secure a deal to be the first cellular provider of the iPhone in the United States. Except the iPhone was nearly launched under the Cingular Wireless name—a brand now consigned to history.

In 2004, our client Cingular Wireless had bought AT&T Wireless and renamed it Cingular Wireless. At the time, Cingular was jointly owned by BellSouth and SBC. The next year, SBC bought the original AT&T and rebranded itself as "the new AT&T." And then, the next year, SBC bought out BellSouth and therefore owned Cingular completely.

Shortly after that, a decision was made to rebrand Cingular as the much better-known AT&T. But the AT&T rebranding was scheduled to be completed in August 2007, well after the planned launch of the iPhone on June 29 of that year.

In April 2007 I had a meeting with Randall Stephenson, then the chairman and CEO of AT&T, in his office in San Antonio, Texas. I told him I believed that the iPhone was the most important product launch of any category of the entire decade. It would be a crime, I said, to introduce it at first under the Cingular name and waste all that brand-building capital.

Randall proceeded to take a pad out of his pocket and make a note on it. Then he put it back in his pocket. Agreeing with me, he said he didn't care if someone had to go to FedEx Kinko's and print out banners on the fly to make it happen, but it needed to get done.

Anyone who has participated in a rebranding knows how labor- and time-intensive it is. You have to change out all of the interior and exterior signage on the stores, and all of the related content. You have to completely reskin the website, and craft and execute communications to both your existing customers and the public at large that the change is happening.

The next day, I heard that the rebranding of Cingular had been brought forward by eight weeks. And in that way the credit associated with the most important product of the decade accrued entirely to AT&T rather than to the now-obscure Cingular name.

Back then, one company in particular was completely blindsided by Apple: BlackBerry, which became a client of ours in 2012. The rise and fall of the BlackBerry is a cautionary tale of what happens when you fail to anticipate the next era in your industry.

What's incredible is that in 1999, BlackBerry had been the one introducing a revolutionary new device: a smartphone *with* a physical keyboard—*and* a trackball. The phone could send texts and emails in addition to making calls. People loved it.

For a time, BlackBerrys rode a technological and cultural wave, with the phones becoming status symbols among businesspeople and celebrities. Because people couldn't seem to stop checking them, the phones were known as crackberries, and *Psychology Today* even ran an article about how to break free of your BlackBerry addiction.[9] (One tip: "Tell yourself I own the BlackBerry, it doesn't own me.")

Up on the stage that day in 2007, Steve Jobs said, "There's an old Wayne Gretsky quote I love—'I skate to where the puck is going to be, not to where it's been.' That's what we try to do at Apple." It's one of the few unoriginal things Jobs ever said, and it's also ironic, because Jim Balsillie, then the cash-flush co-CEO of BlackBerry, had recently tried and failed to buy the Pittsburgh Penguins ice hockey team and move them to Canada, where BlackBerry was based.

There's a great fictional scene in the 2023 movie *Black-Berry* that illustrates how completely the company failed to see where the puck was going (notwithstanding Balsillie's love of hockey).[10] In it, co-CEO Mike Lazaridis (played by Jay Baruchel) gives a presentation to a group of telecom executives in New York on the newest version of the BlackBerry.

He boasts that the device has "the world's first trackpad, which we believe will be the dominant navigational device for all mobile devices within the next two years."

There's a deathly silence in the room before the top telecom executive says, "That's it? That's what you've got for us? A trackpad? You guys see Apple's thing? Any reaction to that?"

Lazaridis tries to dismiss the iPhone as an "overdesigned, trying-to-do-too-much toy that will crash any network gullible enough to take it on. . . . It's by every metric the exact opposite of everything we do."

(Exactly.)

"They put a keyboard right on the screen," the executive points out.

But people love the BlackBerry keyboard and the clicking sound it makes, Lazaridis insists, and then adds, "This entire market was born of our innovation, our idea to put a keyboard on a phone."

"We were kind of hoping you'd come in here with an iPhone killer," says the telecom executive.

At which point an increasingly rattled Lazaridis claims that BlackBerry is working on a top-secret phone with a touchscreen that will retain that satisfying click.

The executives are not impressed.

After Jobs introduced the iPhone, BlackBerry held on for a while longer, but then its stock and its market share began an irrevocable slide. BlackBerry's share of the US smartphone market fell from nearly 50 percent at its peak in 2010 to 0 percent in 2022. That's when the company finally pulled the plug on the legacy services it was offering to the few people who were still clinging to their old phones, which BlackBerry had stopped making in 2016.

As a 2013 article in *Time* magazine noted, BlackBerry's inability to keep up with Apple, and also Google, "was a consequence of errors in its strategy and vision."[11] After seizing the corporate market, BlackBerry did not understand that consumers would drive the next wave of smartphone growth. They were unprepared for the arrival of the "app economy," and the need to ease the way for developers to build apps for their platforms. BlackBerry only ever imagined smartphones as mere communication devices rather than the complete work and entertainment hubs we now know them to be.

After the iPhone came out, we at BBDO saw that even the best advertising in the world would be unable to maintain BlackBerry's market share. Users had fallen hard for the Apple touchscreen. There was no way that BlackBerry would be able to go head-to-head with it on experience and functionality.

When they were still our client, we tried valiantly to get Black-Berry to see the writing on the wall and take a different path. We had found out that agents working for MI6 in Britain used BlackBerrys because their advanced encryption technology made them incredibly secure.

We said: Why not appeal to people for whom privacy and security matter a great deal? If we could say BlackBerrys were so secure that they were the go-to phone for secret agents, it could be a big selling point.

But we couldn't convince them. Who knows? Maybe if they had listened to us, they could have held on to at least 15 percent of the smartphone market instead of zero.

BlackBerry lives on as a company, but not as a phone. John Chen, who took over as CEO in 2013, did realize that the company could not possibly compete with Apple or Google on phone technology.

As he explained in a Harvard Business School case study, "We had been iconic, and we had lost that status. Incremental changes were not going to allow the company to survive and become iconic again. We needed to re-architect the whole company."[12]

Massive layoffs needed to occur because of the company's precarious financial state, but the company was able to successfully transform itself from a hardware to a software company, making use of the powerful network security features that had been a major strength of the BlackBerry phone. By focusing on cybersecurity, encryption, and cryptology, it shifted into a new realm—where it faces a new set of competitors, including Microsoft, Cisco, Citrix, and also Google. Because the competitive creative cycle never ends.

BIG SCARY IDEAS

An ad we did for GE, as part of its "Imagination at Work" campaign, illustrates how people tend to shy away from creative leaps. It shows a life-size, bedraggled puppet-creature with sad eyes, the embodiment of a new idea, wandering the city as others look at him with fear and suspicion.

"Ideas are scary," says the announcer. "They come into the world ugly and messy."

"But under the proper care, they become something beautiful," the announcer continues, as the poor creature, after almost dying on the street, finally receives a warm welcome and a helping hand at the GE offices, where with the proper care he becomes healthier and grows beautiful colorful feathers that he shows off to an audience that gives him a standing ovation.

This twenty-first-century ad is very much in the spirit of Thomas Edison, who was one of the founders of GE back in the nineteenth century. "I find out what the world needs," Thomas Edison said. "Then I go ahead and try to invent it." One of the things he went ahead and invented was the light bulb, now a universal symbol of a creative new idea.

It's somewhat mind-boggling to consider that GE has been BBDO's client since 1920, when Edison was still alive. Some of our earliest campaigns for them included "Live

Better Electrically" and "Progress Is Our Most Important Product." BBDO also came up with the famed "We Bring Good Things to Life," which ran throughout Jack Welch's tenure as CEO from 1981 to 2001.

Welch thrived with an operating model built around Six Sigma—a data-driven approach aimed at improving business processes and reducing defects. Welch emphasized acquisitions and divestments based on a GE asset's financial viability, but there was a limit to how long that strategy would work. After Welch retired in 2001, the new CEO, Jeff Immelt, felt that the company needed a new foundational idea that would stress a new direction for the company.

Jeff happened to take over as chief executive of GE on Monday, September 10, 2001. That night he flew to Seattle for a meeting with one of the company's best customers, Boeing. In his book *Hot Seat*, he describes turning on the TV above a stair climber at the gym the next morning and seeing flames at the top of the North Tower of the World Trade Center.[13] At first he thought a small private plane had flown into the tower. But then a second plane hit the South Tower, and he recognized it as a Boeing 767. Then a third plane struck the Pentagon, and a fourth crashed in Pennsylvania.

As Jeff wrote, "This was gut wrenching for the nation." Talk about an unknown unknown. And on his first week as CEO of GE, it required urgent action on his part. "We'd soon learn that GE was connected to nearly every part of the tragedy," he wrote. "Planes powered by GE engines had just destroyed real estate that was insured by GE-held policies.

The TV network I was watching—NBC—was owned by GE." And two GE people had died in the tragedy.

After his initial trial by fire, Jeff faced one crisis after another. In particular, the company was buffeted by accounting changes as a result of financial fallout from the Enron scandal, in which a massive accounting fraud led to the company's downfall. Then came the 2008 financial crisis. He had to instill discipline and focus inside a company that contained a large number of diverse businesses, from appliances to jet engines to NBC to GE Capital.

Jeff knew that running GE the way Jack Welch had run it was simply not sustainable. "If you've got a company that all it's going to do is go quarter to quarter, that's going to work until it doesn't," Jeff said in a recent interview.[14] "And I guarantee you, there's a time where it won't."

As part of its effort to change direction, GE did its own version of a Creative Shift. The goal was to communicate the GE of today and tomorrow. The company did an enormous amount of research internally and externally, including bringing in ethnographers to define what GE really was as a company.

Jeff has publicly acknowledged that his legacy at GE is complicated, and his exit from the company, in 2017, was unceremonious. But, as he often says, "Truth = Facts + Context." The facts are there for all to see, but not everyone understands the full context of the challenges he faced on multiple fronts.

It was inevitable that some of Jeff's decisions would come in for criticism. But his "Imagination at Work" initiative was one of his strongest plays. It is a perfect example of a Creative Shift, and it became as much a part of the GE way as Six Sigma had been.

"'Bring Good Things to Life' was a great campaign for a long time," Jeff recalled. "But it was essentially a consumer campaign. And we wanted to be more of a technology company."

Some people questioned the need to retire a line that was so well known. After all, a CEO change doesn't necessarily require a marketing change. But the new idea that BBDO helped GE come up with was about much more than marketing. It was about establishing an entirely new model for the company's growth, one that stressed breakthrough ideas and inventions over acquisitions and cost-cutting.

We knew from the start that the word "imagination" needed to be part of the new campaign. Disney had named the workers at its theme parks Imagineers, and that was the kind of creativity we sought to emulate, though in an entirely different realm.

At first we came up with "Imagine That" to express the shift. But then, after writing several TV scripts around the phrase, we discovered that it was already copyrighted by a tiny company nobody had ever heard of. So it was back to the drawing board.

I vividly remember meeting in the Rockefeller Center office of Beth Comstock, then GE's chief marketing officer. Along with a small group that included Beth and the BBDO creative leads Michael Patti and Don Schneider, we used markers to write various forms of the word "Imagine" on big pieces of cardboard. Then we wrote down other words that might partner well with "Imagine" and its siblings.

Sitting on Beth's wonderfully plush carpet (I could easily have taken a nap on it) we looked like toddlers moving the pieces around and around in various combinations.

Finally the right combination clicked together: "Imagination at Work." Beth loved it, and it turned out not to be copyrighted. And as is sometimes the case, the new version was actually much better than the one we'd originally planned to use. Because work—hard work—is a key element of GE's culture.

Building on this powerful idea, Jeff would hold sessions on what he called Imagination Breakthroughs, which gave people opportunities to turn bold new ideas into revenue streams. "These would be projects that were on the boundary," he said in the interview. "And we made sure that they got time and money and attention so they could escape the boundaries that existed inside the company."

One of these efforts, called Ecomagination, was launched in 2005 with the aim of creating sustainable technologies that would both protect the environment and make money for GE. This was long before environmental, social, and governance (ESG) initiatives became popular among corporations. By 2015, the effort had generated $200 billion in revenue.

One idea that came out of Ecomagination was the LEAP engine (for "Leading Edge Aviation Propulsion"), a more sustainable engine than its predecessor that is broadly used by airlines today. The effort also resulted in partnerships with companies including Statoil, Total, Goldman Sachs, Walmart, and Intel that were designed to reduce greenhouse gases, environmental waste, and water pollution and spur renewable energy, among other things.

"Imagination at Work" also led to the development of new technologies that enabled the cleanup of pollution in the Hudson River, much of which had come from GE plants. "We pivoted from being kind of the polluter-of-record to implementing the biggest clean-tech initiative at that time," Jeff recalled.

Another "Imagination at Work" effort, called Healthymagination, helped the company expand beyond big healthcare machines like MRIs, CT scans, and X-rays and into precision diagnostics via smaller devices and software.

What GE's engineers, scientists, and factory workers do is rigorous and precise—and difficult. "It's really hard to create a wind blade the size of a football field and make sure that it works," Linda Boff, a former GE chief marketing officer, said recently.[15] "It's really hard to create medical equipment that fits in your hand. It's hard to create jet engines that work every single time." "Imagination at Work" respected that, while helping the company open itself up to more experimentation, playfulness, and outright humor.

Some remarkable technological breakthroughs came out of those imagination sessions, and at BBDO we used them as the basis for stories in our campaign.

In one commercial to go along with the campaign, GE Robots are seen snoring, reading the paper, and playing cards because their jobs painting cars have been rendered obsolete by a new type of plastic invented by GE. Sadly, the now-idle robots are ordered to report immediately to the crash-testing facility.

In another, a baby elephant is shown tap dancing, splashing, and trumpeting its way through a verdant rainforest to the tune of "Singin' in the Rain," as a parrot, a toucan, a chimpanzee, and a pair of flamingos look on. The announcer says, "Water that's more pure. Jet engines, trains, and power plants that run dramatically cleaner. At GE we're using what we call Ecomagination to create technology that's right in step with nature."

The "Imagination at Work" campaign has come and gone, but its impact was permanent and wide ranging. It encouraged swing-for-the-fences ideas, some of which worked and some of which didn't. Still more Creative Shifts may well lie ahead now that GE has split into three separate companies, one focusing on aerospace, another on energy, and a third on health care.

At BBDO, we work with companies like GE that consistently generate and execute on really big ideas while managing a healthy business. New ideas scare, frustrate, and irritate us, too, but we've learned to work with them in a business environment alongside metrics, budgets, and deadlines. As professional creatives, we know how to wall the idea development function off from the rest of a business: the profit planning meetings, the forecasting and budgeting processes, and the hiring interviews.

One of our defined strategies at BBDO has been to secure an unfair share of the limited pool of exceptional creative talent on the planet. Talent is a point of pride for us. That said, talent isn't what stands between organizations and better ideas. The *who* is only a part of our creative success. BBDO is the most awarded agency on Earth because of *how* our people work. In advising some of the biggest companies in the world, I've seen that any organization can reliably leverage creativity once it learns to manage the process.

2

THE WORKOUT

The great David Abbott, a legendary copywriter and one of the founders of Abbott Mead Vickers, the agency that became AMV BBDO in London, used to say, "There isn't an advertising problem in the world that can't be solved in two days if you put the right people on it. But please don't tell anybody."

Maybe he was being too optimistic, but not by much. I'm convinced that *if* you've laid all the groundwork, then you can emerge with a truly great, extremely creative idea in several days.

But that's a big if. And it's why so many organizations fail to achieve a true Creative Shift. That is exactly why we designed the two- to three-day creative sessions that we call WorkOuts.

First things first, though: Before you embark on a Work-Out, you need to do plenty of research and anthropological foraging, and let all your insights soak in your brain, consciously and unconsciously.

Then you need to come up with an extremely well-defined question to answer or problem to solve. Next, you need to devise a series of prompts—specific cues designed to get the creative process going—based on the defined problem.

Then: You need to have the right people working on the problem. You might think that means only including the people you have identified as "experts." And yes, you do need experts. But you *also* need to include people who have almost no expertise in the matter at hand.

You bring this varied group of people together for a few days, preferably outside of their usual surroundings. And you ensure that this is the *only* thing they work on over this period, in a highly structured way.

Then comes the really hard part, because it flies in the face of how people think problems should be attacked. It involves a kind of mental jiu jitsu that is highly foreign to most people's way of problem-solving. You must actively encourage everyone in the group to generate as many *bad* ideas as they possibly can.

Be bad. Be stupid. Be wrong. Now, do it again. And again. And again. And again.

Which is the idea behind BBDO's WorkOuts. Because what happens after that is magic.

Even though brainstorming was in the original DNA of BBDO, it started to fade in the 1970s and 1980s as people put more emphasis on creating perfect scripts for TV commercials, which tends to be more of a solo than a collaborative effort. Even at BBDO, brainstorming was often reduced to making improvements rather than coming up with genuinely original ideas.

But around the turn of the century, advertising started to expand at a rapid pace into whole new platforms, thanks to the explosion of the internet and electronic devices. We needed the collective creativity of our agency's talent, not just the craftsmanship of individuals, to adapt to this new reality.

Toward that end, I commissioned Peter Souter and Danny Searle, who were part of the five-person BBDO Worldwide Creative Committee, to come up with a BBDO process for creating ideas.

And so the WorkOut came to life. The aim was to take advantage of BBDO's size, strength, and breadth to come up with big, bold, creative new ideas for our advertisers—and do it efficiently.

When I recently asked Peter to talk about WorkOuts, he quickly wrote up a description of how they operate and sent it to me in an email. As it pretty much encapsulates their essence, I'll just let him take the floor, as he would do for us so brilliantly at BBDO time and again.

The WorkOut is BBDO's way of putting real brains into the brainstorm process. It's founded on two principles of collaboration: A good idea doesn't mind who has it. And none of us are as smart as all of us.

When there's a big problem or, better still, a big opportunity, we call a WorkOut. We invite everybody with skin in the game. Writers, art directors, planners, business leads, producers, and, whenever possible, the client.

I like to have the client come three times:

1. The bon voyage. Once at the start. The last piece of advice David Abbott gave me was "always read the client's brief." I like to go one further and have them come to the first hour of the WorkOut and tell us, face to face, what the dream outcome looks like.

Sometimes I give them a little toy fairy wand and say, "Imagine if absolutely everything about your business was going great—what would that look like?"

Once they've briefed us to their heart's content, we politely ask them to go. Creation is ugly. You need to think of a LOT of bad ideas to get to a great one. And that's not a spectator sport. True, some clients want to stay. But most understand and leave us to it.

2. The mid-Atlantic. Visit two is at the halfway stage. We put on a conversation-only show of how it's been going. But no formal executions. Just loose areas. The dream of what an idea might be. Then, again, we invite them to leave.

In more recent times I've been throwing up an Instagram page for the group, including the client, where I'll take pictures and scribble Post-it-note-style ideas into a mosaic for them to comment on. This can be soothing (they can see that stuff is happening and sometimes their comments can be helpful). It's a nightly chore but it seems popular and useful.

3. The wrap party. The last visit, obviously, is the most important. The WorkOut group creates an "exhibition," a walk-in visualization of our collective brains and what they've thought up (of which more in a moment).

There's another reason to bring the client in those three times.

When I took my kids to a fish restaurant when they were little, they always ran straight up to the tank and named all the lobsters in there. That way, I couldn't eat them. They were Chuck and Bob and Lizzy. Not food anymore.

A great reason to involve the client deeply in the process is that they see us caring about their business. Deeply. They see the full might of BBDO coming together to make them money. More than that, to make them matter.

Andrew always used to say that, even on the rare occasion the WorkOut doesn't work, it's still a magnificent gesture. Consummate account management. And I always used to say, "But the WorkOut *always* works."

Okay, speeding up: Here's what a BBDO WorkOut is like when the client isn't there.

The space. I hate doing WorkOuts in the agency. It's not special enough. People keep scurrying away to do their day job, and that breaks the spell. So generally speaking we rent a brilliant Airbnb or a cool boutique hotel and take it over. Everyone hangs out all the time, coming together for group sessions. The space allows people to hide away and think when they need to. Extroverts need people, introverts need space. Any team will have both, so you need to be aware of that deep creative need for one or the other.

The materials. In this digital world sometimes it's great to go totally analog. So I run WorkOuts as all-paper events. All you need for a WorkOut is a ton of big Post-its, some big white foam boards to stick them on, and lots of pens to scribble on them with.

And food. If you've got French people in the team they need to be fed five times a day with the highest-quality food and excellent wine. Or they start building guillotines and looking at you darkly. Non-French people aren't much better. An army marches on its stomach and all that.

The discipline. WorkOuts are meant to be scary. Tight deadlines, public ideas, incoming clients. All of these are good things. Great thinkers love appreciation. Even the introverts. And truly great people thrive under pressure. Not too much. That just makes folks cry. But a little pressure, a little healthy competition, a little professional pride all help the chemistry of a WorkOut. Time is healthy pressure, the approval of your peers is healthy pressure, a client you care about and who trusts you enough to pay for a WorkOut—all of these help people to do their best work, in my humble opinion.

The rules:

Yes, plus (or yes, and). Nobody craps on anything until very near the end. If someone shares an idea, you go, "Interesting, what about if we build on that by doing this . . ." Yes plus leans to ideas that grow. "No, that won't work" means the whole process dies on its ass immediately. There's a time for judgment, but at the beginning you water the flowers, you don't step on them.

Everything is a Post-it. If it won't fit on a Post-it, it won't work on a poster. If you can't get it down to something simple, it's too complicated to sell. I make everyone put their Macs away and create something tangible. Post-its can be moved around easily. Edited. Improved. Ticked and crossed out. They also don't get lost in someone's laptop.

Let the room be your creative director. Every night I give everyone in the room ten colorful sticky dots and ask them to stick them on the ideas they like. It's a really great way to get a feel for the thoughts that everyone likes. It doesn't always work, but, generally speaking, if it's a great idea, everybody senses it. It also helps edit out ideas without seeming to favor teams, disciplines, or countries. The room just loves great ideas. Nobody is picking on you if you don't have one. Just think of better ideas tomorrow.

Play games. It's important to be playful. All creativity is, essentially, play. So we try to "gamify" the early beats of a WorkOut. For example, the "words, pictures, insights" game is an attempt to crack the challenge at its most basic level. Everybody plays, regardless of discipline. You have an hour and three colors of Post-its. Then you try to solve the client's problem in a sentence, a picture, or an insight. One sentence that perfectly captures the essence of the brand. One insight that sums up what the consumer is feeling right now. And one picture that illustrates the spirit of the brand. It's basically fun. But I can't tell you how often people come up with the killer endline in this game. It's amazing.

The timetable. I like this rhythm: Go wide, go narrow, go deep, go public. I divide the time up into quarters, encourage people to be free and outrageous, then try to narrow things down, then get the "room" to choose three great routes, then have everyone go deep and fill out the skeleton idea until it lives and breathes.

The exhibition. Then we create the walk-through exhibition that I mentioned and put on a show for the client. In my experience there's no better presenter than the people who created the idea. So we all take part in the presentation.

Thanks to people like Peter, though, it never feels like a presentation. As Chris Beresford-Hill, who took over from David Lubars as global chief creative officer of BBDO Worldwide, put it to me recently, "The agency and the client stand shoulder to shoulder, facing the same wall of strategy and ideas. You are no longer 'presenter' and 'receiver,' you are teammates, solving the problem together."

THE LEGACY OF THE *O*

At BBDO, I haven't been too fond of celebrating the past. I think it's much more important to keep all eyes on the present and the future. But the fact is, where we came from has played a big part in who we are now. And that's true of our WorkOuts, even though we lost sight of that for a time.

As I mentioned earlier, in 1928 the George Batten advertising company merged with the Barton, Durstine, and Osborn agency, along with their names. It's the O of the quartet—Alex Osborn—who has left the most lasting mark on the agency, and on the whole field of organizational psychology. He actually invented and popularized the concept of brainstorming.

Today, some academics say the technique doesn't work. Their research shows that individuals generate more ideas working alone than they do together.

Adam Grant, the author and organizational psychology professor, threw cold water on the concept of brainstorming in a 2023 article for *Time*:

Think about the brainstorming sessions you've attended. You've probably seen people bite their tongues due to ego threat ("I don't want to look stupid"), noise ("We can't all talk at once."), and conformity pressure ("Let's all jump on the boss's bandwagon!"). Goodbye diversity of thought, hello groupthink. These challenges are amplified for people who lack power or status: the most junior person in the room, the sole woman of color in a team of bearded white dudes, the introvert drowning in a sea of extraverts.[1]

Speaking as a practitioner, I can tell you that Professor Grant is describing badly run brainstorming. Yes, if you just sit a group of people around a table and say, "What are your ideas on growing our business?" and set up no ground rules or structure, then the effort is almost certainly doomed to fail.

Brainstorming has stood the test of time at BBDO because it works under a specific set of rules, under pressure, and on a deadline.

As Alex Osborn said, "Creativity is more than mere imagination. It is imagination inseparably coupled with both intent and effort."[2]

We're paid to deliver big ideas on demand, and we get the job done. It comes down to technique. The key to *effective* brainstorming is to deconstruct the problem by clearing away all the assumptions and conventions, assembling a team with at least a few outsiders, and assigning a competent facilitator. Without those elements, you're just spitballing.

And crucially, as Osborn wrote, brainstorming should operate on "the principle of suspended judgment." This is a key point that many critics of brainstorming miss. The group leader "must always insist that the ideas produced be judged not during the brainstorming session—but afterward," he said.

Jony Ive, who helped design one of the greatest products of all time, the iPhone, understands this deeply. Speaking to graduates of the California College of the Arts in 2021, he said, "Ideas, by definition, are always fragile. If they were resolved, they wouldn't be ideas. They would be products that were ready to ship. I've come to learn that you have to make an extraordinary effort not to focus on the problems which are implicated with any new idea. These problems are known, they're quantifiable and understood, but you have to focus on the actual idea, which is partial, tentative, and unproven. If you don't actively suspend your disbelief, if you don't believe there is a solution to the problems, of course you'll lose faith in your idea. That is why criticism and focusing on the problems can be so damaging, particularly in the absence of a constructive idea."[3]

Suspending judgment is central to the "yes, and . . ." approach that is a major pillar of improvisational comedy. Tina Fey honed the method when she was a member of the storied Second City comedy troupe. She describes how "yes, and . . ." works, and the philosophy behind it, in her book *Bossypants*:

> The first rule of improvisation is AGREE. Always agree and SAY YES. When you're improvising, this

means you are required to agree with whatever your partner has created. . . .

As an improviser, I always find it jarring when I meet someone in real life whose first answer is no. "No, we can't do that." "No, that's not in the budget." "No, I will not hold your hand for a dollar." What kind of way is that to live?[4]

The second rule of improvisation, after agreeing, is to contribute something yourself. In fact, Fey says, it is your *responsibility* to contribute. If she starts out by saying, "I can't believe it's so hot in here," and the other person just says, "Yeah," then the whole scene pretty much ends right there. But if the other person says, "What did you expect? We're in hell," Fey says, or "Yes, this can't be good for the wax figures," or "I told you we shouldn't have crawled into this dog's mouth," then you're on your way.

The third rule, Fey continues, is to make statements. Don't put all the pressure on other people to come up with answers. In other words, she advises, "Whatever the problem, be part of the solution."

And the fourth rule is there are no mistakes. Channeling the prolific and mesmerizing public-television painter Bob Ross, Fey says that there are "only beautiful happy accidents." An example: "If I start a scene as what I think is very clearly a cop riding a bicycle, but you think I am a hamster in a hamster wheel, guess what? Now I'm a hamster in a hamster wheel. I'm not going to stop everything to explain that was really supposed to be a bike. Who knows? Maybe I'll end up being a police hamster who's been put on 'hamster wheel' duty."

RUNNING OUT OF TIME

Now, you could end up running on a kind of endless creative hamster wheel if you kept spouting ideas without a time limit. All those ideas need some kind of time constraint. In short, a deadline. Time pressure is a good kind of fear that keeps the creative process moving and heading toward concrete action.

When people talk about how time pressure sparks creativity, they sometimes bring up the Apollo 13 disaster of 1970, where an explosion in an oxygen tank released deadly carbon dioxide into the crew cabin. The three astronauts would have died before returning to Earth if NASA engineers had not invented, under the most severe pressure, an improvised air filtration system using items they knew were on the spacecraft (including duct tape and technical manuals), and that they were reasonably sure a trio of carbon dioxide–addled astronauts could duplicate. The jerry-built invention would never win any design prizes, but it brought the astronauts back alive, a feat so miraculous that Ron Howard made an Academy Award–winning movie out of it.

We all know people who shine under the pressure of a deadline. David Abbott was one of them. Once when we were about to make a huge Volvo presentation, we reviewed all the work the day before the meeting, and all of it was dreadful. We all felt pretty hopeless. David was very disappointed.

The next day we walked in and David presented fifteen brilliantly written ads that he'd done overnight. The deadline was the thing that had driven him into action.

However, "when creativity is under the gun, it usually ends up getting killed," say researchers Teresa Amabile, Constance Hadley, and Steven Kramer in an article for *Harvard Business Review*.[5] "Although time pressure may drive people to work more and get more done, and may even make them feel more creative, it actually causes them, in general, to think less creatively." But, they hasten to add, there is more to the story.

The researchers conducted a study in which they asked the participants—most of them knowledge workers—to keep a diary while they worked on projects that required a high degree of creativity and that also had varying degrees of time pressure. Working off the diaries, they developed a "Time-Pressure Creativity Matrix."

When there is little to no time pressure, the researchers discovered, creativity is unlikely to thrive: "People feel as if they are on autopilot" and "engage in less collaborative work overall," among other things. On the other side of the matrix, when time pressure is intense, creative ideas are also unlikely to emerge: People feel as if they are on a treadmill—particularly if they constantly feel distracted, if their days become fragmented, and if plans, schedules, and deadlines keep changing.

But in some situations extreme time pressure actually spurs creativity. This is "when people feel they are on a mission," said the researchers. This is literally what happened with the astronauts and engineers of Apollo 13. To quote again from Amabile and her colleagues, deadlines spur creativity when people:

- can focus on one activity for a significant part of the day because they are undisturbed or protected.
- believe that they are doing important work and report feeling positively challenged by and involved in the work.
- show creative thinking that is equally oriented toward identifying problems and generating or exploring ideas.

True creativity under extreme time pressure is rare but possible, the researchers assert. Above all, people need to be able to focus on a single task, and they need to be protected from interruptions while pursuing a project of "meaningful urgency."

As the brilliant Nancy Reyes, who succeeded me as chief executive officer of BBDO Worldwide, put it so beautifully when we discussed it, "Creativity doesn't need a lot of time, just the space to be randomly inspired and the freedom to be spontaneous."

Exactly the conditions that exist in our WorkOuts.

THE SMELL OF AN APP

Back in 2019, I gave Josy Paul, head of BBDO India, a single task to focus on—and it was a big one: Come up with a new foundational campaign idea for WhatsApp, the messaging app owned by Meta.

We agreed that, because we needed an idea that would work around the world, it would be smart to organize a WorkOut with teams of writers and art directors from India, the United States, Mexico, Germany, and Brazil.

On the first day, after the client left the room in Menlo Park, California, Josy asked the teams that had gathered there an important question:

"What does WhatsApp smell like?"

Josy said later he was afraid he would get sacked for asking such an out-of-left-field question—one that had only occurred to him that morning.

Josy had participated in WorkOuts before, although he had never led one. But I knew he would be perfect for the Meta campaign, and I was right. And I can assure you that he was never in danger of being sacked.

A WorkOut enables you to accomplish something in three days that might normally take twenty-one days, Josy said from Mumbai.[6] "You're doing it with people you don't know, and the diversity forces new collisions and new possibilities." There's a sense of sharing that's almost like a bonfire. "And what happens with the sharing is that there is a sense of equality. Everyone in the room feels comfortable asking questions. And everyone in the room can share whatever they think is the answer."

We do have a template for our WorkOuts, but all of our moderators are free to bring their own creativity and sensibilities to the process, depending on the needs of the client and their sense of what's happening in the room.

At the time that Josy led that WorkOut, WhatsApp already had 2 billion users around the globe (it now has close to 3 billion), and Josy felt that kind of reach required a whole different approach to advertising. The idea had occurred to him that day to go beyond information and create ideas around the five senses. He wanted to evoke feelings, not provide information. Hence his "crazy" question.

And as it turned out, the BBDO creatives who had gathered from all over the world *were* able to imagine and express what WhatsApp smelled like to them. Josy wrote their responses on pieces of paper and pinned them to a board at the front of the room. Here are some of their answers.

- Sunday Roast (Remembering my family)
- Someone cooking something hot
- Ginger tea; leather couch
- Homey, fresh, "mum-washed" bed sheets
- FART! (SORRY)

Later people placed round purple stickers on the answers that resonated most with them, and guess what? "FART" got the most stickers.

Was the word FART weird? Yes. Unpleasant? Yes. Insightful? Massively.

As the person who came up with that answer explained, you are truly close to someone if you feel free to let one loose in front of them in the privacy of your own home. And that was the kind of feeling that WhatsApp wanted to convey with its ads.

Now, none of the ads that later emerged as a result of that WorkOut featured farts (and that's probably for the best), but I think the fact that someone felt secure enough to come up with that unexpected answer, and to share it with the whole room, says a lot about the power of the WorkOut.

The group came up with the following goal: "To establish a clear, uniquely differentiated value proposition around privacy that creates a lasting emotional connection with users, and ultimately builds equity that protects us against harm, people switching to other apps, helps introduce new product bets."

And they decided the campaign would seek to illuminate three major, overlapping elements: intimate relationships, human truth, and product magic.

Josy then asked the teams to tell a very short story about what WhatsApp meant to them.

Some of the offerings:

- My grandparents slept hand in hand for 70 years
- Two people alone in silence
  a shared experience
  no need to talk
  just knowing someone's there
- Baseball players making signs

- Me and my colleague share a silent look when the client says something we don't agree with

He also asked them to evoke WhatsApp with a symbol, a color, a film scene, and a drawing (no drawing ability required—stick figures were just fine).

After all of this drawing and writing and imagining, all the teams were asked to write a "manifesto" that encapsulated the feelings and ideas they had come up with.

The Mexican team's manifesto went like this:

Everybody has a different way to say things
The stories you tell by the conversations you have
The messages you send
That's the beauty about talking to each other
What you say, says who you are
And how you say it, is only yours
That emoji that means nothing to everybody, but
    everything to you
The sticker you created with your boss's face
That meme that tells your girlfriend how you feel
    better than words
Those are the things that belong to you and to
    nobody else
The thing that makes you and your people feel
    together
What brings us closer
Your inside jokes
Your personal memories

Your everyday conversations
Between you and your friends, your mother, your
    teacher, your lover
And they stay where they should stay
Where they were born.
WhatsApp
Between you

And there it was. The kernel that led to the successful world-wide WhatsApp campaign with the theme "It's between you." Three words that had a double meaning, connoting both intimacy and an assurance of privacy.

At the end of the second day of the WorkOut, Josy brought in a professional artist to create colorful, poster-worthy images representing what he and the group considered to be the strongest foundational concepts to emerge from the WorkOut. At the end of the third day, these were presented to the client, and "Between You" emerged as the clear favorite.

Shortly after that WorkOut the COVID-19 pandemic hit, quickly followed by the lockdown, and the agency had to film the commercials in the actors' homes, often with their relatives holding the camera. Many of these ads went on to win awards, and Josy said he was so proud of them that he had the feeling afterward that "one can die after this."

The restrictions on filming gave an air of homey intimacy to the ads. In one of the TV ads that aired in India starting in July 2020, at the height of the pandemic, an elderly woman is shown communicating with her caregiver, Nurse

Anita, in their separate homes. The distinctive sound of the WhatsApp chime signals a continuing conversation between the two. At the end, the two women blow kisses at each other over the phone, and the words "What brings you together, is between you" appear on the screen, signaling the double meaning: that the app enables closeness between two people while also ensuring their privacy with end-to-end encryption.

In another ad that aired in India, a woman who is distressed about her straggly pandemic hair gets on a video call with her sister, who talks her through how to give herself a haircut, pantomiming with her fingers how to hold the scissors. The woman is nervous, but she takes a deep breath and starts cutting, and the ends of her black locks start accumulating on a table. The end result is a success, the woman's face beams, and the sister whistles her congratulations. The words, "What gives you courage, is between you," appear on the screen. Cue the WhatsApp chime.

The WhatsApp ad in Germany starts out with a couple arguing and then both of them leaving, upset, for their separate jobs. While at work they each check their phones, first expectant, then despondent, and they don't hear anything from each other until the woman is home and the man is just outside their door with a bouquet of flowers. He finally texts her, and when she hears the chime of his text, she opens the door. Then they continue texting sweet messages (which the viewer can't see, because they're private). Cue the chime: "What brings you close again, is between you."

WorkOuts are a way to steadily alternate between divergence and convergence. As Josy put it, "Groups of people from different countries who have never met each other, and who have different professional backgrounds, bring about new collisions of ideas and new possibilities."

COOPERATION OVER COMPETITION

Our London agency, AMV BBDO, won the Guinness advertising account for Great Britain and Ireland, the beer's biggest-volume region, in 1998, and it went on to do some extraordinary work on the brand. Later we picked up the account in the United States. Another agency, Saatchi & Saatchi, was responsible for Africa, the second most important region, and also Asia. Each region came up with its own campaign ideas.

But then the people at Diageo, the brand owner, decided they wanted a single global campaign idea. They planned to pitch the account between us and Saatchi & Saatchi—winner takes all. Before that could happen, I went to Diageo with a proposal: Bring your two trusted agencies together to create a single global platform idea, and use a WorkOut to do it.

As Danny Searle, the chief creative officer for BBDO Asia at the time, recalled recently in an email, "It was hard for the clients to disagree with this logic. And the other agency couldn't really say no."

So it was decided that a WorkOut would be organized, to be jointly run by Danny and the Saatchi & Saatchi creative director. The two rival agencies ended up working together—in a small hotel in the Irish countryside—for three days straight. After a thorough analysis, they came up with a brief: "A beer of substance. For a man of substance."

The team played nicely together. And at the end of the three days, they had three very good ideas that they were ready to present to Diageo in London. But, as Danny recalled, "On the way back, as we were reading through the notes to set up the presentation, we noted we had written the line 'Made with More.' And with a small but significant tweak, it became 'Made of More.' And we knew we had it. And the client did too."

But it wasn't until BBDO released an American ad called "Wheelchairs" that it knew it had cracked the code, Danny said. That ad became one of the most awarded TV campaigns in the world.

In the ad written by Chris Beresford-Hill, six men in wheelchairs play a sweaty, punishing game of basketball in a gym, with a few of the chairs actually tipping over. At the end of the game, five of the men get out of their wheelchairs and walk to the exit with their friend who actually needs to use a wheelchair. Later the six friends are shown at the pub sharing glasses of Guinness. "Dedication, loyalty, friendship," the announcer says. "The choices we make reveal the true nature of our character." And on the screen: "Made of More."

Over the years, BBDO found that WorkOuts had other benefits besides speeding up the process, especially for big regional or global campaigns. In a WorkOut, every market could be included in the process, as with the WhatsApp example I referred to earlier. This had two important advantages. First, the ideas were stress-tested for local relevance as they were being developed, not after the event. And second, they were collectively owned because everyone was present at the conception.

"The WorkOut enabled BBDO to compete against the much bigger, established agencies across Asia," where BBDO was a latecomer, Danny said. In every market, BBDO was smaller than the agencies it was competing against—sometimes those agencies had ten times as many employees. "So they could always outgun us—unless we combined our agency resources and turned up as a WorkOut."

The WorkOuts changed everything. "It meant we could have a team, just as big, but much more selective and effective. Handpicked for the specific job," said Danny. "No one agency, even the biggest in Asia, could match the firepower of a BBDO WorkOut. And none of them really knew how to harness their network power like BBDO could. That's how we managed to grow a network so quickly, and punch well above our weight."

Advertising and marketing lore is filled with examples of campaigns that went off the rails because of words and phrases that became hilariously lost in translation. The Swedish company Electrolux, for example, didn't strike quite the right note in America with its "Nothing Sucks Like an Electrolux" campaign for vacuum cleaners. The now-defunct Braniff Airlines, eager to show off its new leather seats in the 1980s, unveiled a campaign centered on the phrase "Fly in leather," not knowing that in some parts of the Spanish-speaking world the translation meant "Fly naked."

And Kentucky Fried Chicken did not make the best first impression when it launched in China in the 1980s by translating its signature phrase "Finger-Lickin' Good" into "Eat Your Fingers Off" in Chinese.

Translation errors are just the tip of the iceberg. As business becomes increasingly globalized, the potential for cultural misunderstandings has only grown, which is one reason why it is so critical to have people from a diverse range of geographic and cultural backgrounds participating in idea-generation sessions. Other reasons are that they expand everyone's notion of what is possible, and can validate the universal appeal of a great foundational idea.

There's no point doing a WorkOut for a single ad campaign, or for an incremental improvement. For these, the more traditional BBDO process of working with a client, briefing our teams, working out the concept, and then presenting it to the client works just fine. But when you need to create a completely new foundational idea, the WorkOut works great.

THE TRANSFORMATION OF BARBIE

"The best success we've had with WorkOuts is when a business is at a crossroads," said Matt Miller, chief creative officer for BBDO on the West Coast of the United States. It's where "we do the big idea."

That was certainly the case when Mattel came to BBDO in 2014. They had a big question: What is the purpose of Barbie? (Or, as Billie Eilish would put it in the song she later wrote for the *Barbie* movie, "What was I made for?")

When Ruth Handler invented the Barbie doll in 1959, she brought about a Creative Shift of her own; it fueled the success of the nascent Mattel toy company that she had formed with her husband and a business partner. Handler saw that there was a dearth of dolls resembling adults on the market, despite a plethora of baby-like dolls that encouraged nurturing. Barbie filled the void, with 300,000 dolls sold in their first year on the market.

Considering that the average life cycle for a toy is three to five years, Barbie's longevity has been exceptional. "For a doll and a brand to transcend generations is a big deal," Lisa McKnight, executive vice president and chief brand officer for Mattel, said recently.[7] But naturally, through the decades you're going to have some highs and lows, she added.

A high came in 2009 when Barbie turned fifty and the company was able to celebrate her as a pop culture icon. But several years later Barbie sales began to decline, and the brand hit a big low.

The problem? "We weren't focusing on a broader message of why Barbie matters," Lisa said. The company's advertising, mainly aimed at kids, focused more on Barbie's features rather than being directed at parents and describing how Barbie might contribute to a child's development.

At the same time, society was embracing a much more diverse view of beauty. Brands like Dove had already recognized this by spotlighting women of all different body types in its "Real Beauty" ads. Barbie, known for her blonde hair, extremely narrow waist, and very long legs, had become disconnected from that.

One piece of research that Mattel did was especially unsettling: Parents who had grown up with Barbie and played with her when they were children no longer saw her as a role model, and they didn't feel comfortable giving her as a gift at children's birthday parties.

Mattel knew they needed to make a foundational shift, but they didn't completely know how. And so they turned to BBDO for help, and BBDO held a WorkOut, led by Matt. What resulted from those three days was about much more than ads.

"We hired BBDO to help us identify the true purpose behind Barbie and help us ground ourselves in that original intention of the brand as a beacon of female empowerment," Lisa said, "because it was always there. Barbie for years has always been a girl's first empowerment experience."

At the Barbie WorkOut, after two days of diverging and converging, going wide and going narrow—with the help of Post-its, pens, big sticky boards, and stickers—Matt and his teams came up with three of their best foundational ideas.

They presented those ideas to the client on the third day, with thoughts on how those ideas could live inside and outside the organization. The idea that resonated the most with Mattel was "Imagine the possibilities," which fit with the brand's "You can be anything" tagline.

"That was when they saw the clarity of the brand," Matt recalled.

From there the concept went to the execution stage, and to a two-minute video that went viral in 2016.

In it, the words "What happens when girls are free to imagine they can be anything?" appear on the screen. The video shows little girls taking on various professional roles in front of bemused and impressed adults (who appear to be taken a bit off guard): professor, veterinarian, sports coach, museum docent, business executive. At the end of the video the camera cuts to one of the little girls speaking as a professor to a group of her Barbies, who all look different from one another.

The video ends with the words, "When a girl plays with Barbie, she imagines everything she could be. You can be anything. Barbie."

The video received millions of views and caused one Facebook commenter to exclaim, "Wow . . . that made me change my mind on Barbie."

Along with the campaign, Mattel got to work on developing over a hundred different expressions of Barbie, with a variety of body types, skin tones, hair fibers, eyes, and face sculpts. The changes received "an incredible endorsement not only from kids but from parents," Lisa said. "Our sales improved dramatically."

The experience was transformative for Mattel. When a WorkOut works, "You leave the room with your big North Star and your anchor," as Matt put it.

On one Post-it toward the end of the Barbie WorkOut, Matt remembers, someone wrote, "This culminates in a major, blockbuster movie."

For decades Mattel had been convinced that Barbie would make a perfect subject for a movie, but the right project never seemed to materialize. Then, in 2018, a documentary called *Tiny Shoulders: Rethinking Barbie*, distributed by Hulu, chronicled the doll's transformation.

Mere weeks after taking on the role of chairman and CEO of Mattel that same year, Ynon Kreiz met with Margot Robbie to share his vision for a *Barbie* movie, and the rest is now Hollywood history. *Barbie* was the highest-grossing movie of 2023. Sales of the doll, of course, exploded even further after the movie was released.

While the movie was a risk for Mattel, as it took satirical aim at the traditional Barbie, it certainly paid off. It involved a certain amount of stepping outside Mattel's comfort zone, but "we knew we were in good hands working with top talent," Lisa said.

Since Mattel's Creative Shift, the company has made it a point to focus on Barbie not just as a toy but as a form of intellectual property. There are now Barbie collaborations spanning over fifty categories, including digital games, hotels, museum exhibits, and restaurants.

Our WorkOuts often influence our clients' products and services—and even their corporate culture. "When you have your purpose and your big idea, it should impact every component of a business," Matt said.

Yes, a WorkOut requires a fairly significant outlay of time and resources, and it forces you to take time away from your day-to-day work. But that's exactly the point. And that's exactly why they work.

3

THE CULTURE OF
THE CREATIVE SHIFT

In business, "culture" is one of those words that, like "inno-vation," can become so watered down that it ends up being meaningless. That's because many business leaders like to define their company's culture in terms of what they want the company to be—and what they think people want to hear—instead of what is actually happening on the ground.

This chapter will describe how company culture can either support, or stifle, creativity. But first, what is your company's culture, *really*?

In order to achieve a successful Creative Shift, a company must first be honest and specific about defining its culture. Otherwise the unspoken and unconscious elements of the culture can take hold in unintended and counterproductive ways, because people read so much more into behavior than into words. And let's face it: At many companies it's not the survival of the fittest, it's the survival of the conformist.

There's an episode of the sitcom *Friends* that hilariously illustrates the effects of unspoken culture. It's the one where, as a new employee, Rachel (one of the six friends) starts to realize that all the important decisions are made when Kim, her boss at Ralph Lauren, is on smoke breaks with Nancy, Rachel's coworker who smokes. As a nonsmoker, Rachel finds herself at a distinct disadvantage.

One day, Kim interrupts a work discussion with Rachel and Nancy to say it's time for a smoke break, and Nancy quickly gets up to join her. As Rachel hangs back, Kim asks her if she smokes, and Rachel says, "Oh, no, my dad's a doctor and he would always tell me horror stories . . . [she stops herself and changes course] about ghosts and goblins . . . who . . . totally supported the princess's right to smoke!"

Later Rachel complains bitterly to her friend Monica about her company's smoking culture. "What if this keeps happening? They'll be outside smoking making all the decisions, and I'll just be up in my office breathing in my stupid clean air. And then when the day comes when Kim wants to promote one of us, who do you think she's going to pick? Me or Smoky Smokerson?"

Monica urges Rachel to join the two women anyway, while Chandler (a third friend) says, "Why don't you just do the easy thing and smoke?"

Not long afterward, Rachel ends up going outside for "some fresh air" while Kim and Nancy are discussing the fall collection on their smoke break. Rachel can't help recoiling after Kim blows smoke in her face, so Kim apologizes, and she and Nancy move away to continue their shoptalk. In frustration, Rachel ends up bumming a cigarette and smoking (with a first-timer's coughing clumsiness) so she can be part of their strategy session.

Later, when Rachel tells Monica how great her day went and how excited her boss was about her ideas, Monica interrupts her to say, "You stink!" Rachel finally admits that she smoked, but she defends herself by saying, "This is actually the smell of success," and "I had to do it for my career!"

That's unconscious culture at work. It clearly had not occurred to Rachel's boss that in effect she was rewarding people who were smokers. But it was so crystal clear to Rachel that she changed her behavior (to the detriment of her own health) to benefit from it.

Company culture is not theoretical and abstract. It is based on the actual behaviors and experiences of the people in the organization.

I have a deep personal sense of this. I was born in Zimbabwe, where my father, after founding and selling a soft-serve ice cream business, eventually became a production manager for Nestlé. When I was nine the company transferred him to South Africa, and nine years later he moved to England, where I joined the family after I finished high school. In 2001 I moved to the United States to take the CEO job at BBDO

North America. At this point, I've lived in the United States longer than anywhere else.

Whenever someone asks where I'm from, I'm never sure how to answer. I've always felt that the best answer would be "from somewhere else," because that's how it's always seemed. Although this is a little disorienting, it's also been a gift. It's helped me adapt, both consciously and unconsciously, to different cultures, and to become very attuned to understanding what a culture is and isn't, including in an organizational context.

Too many companies proclaim what their culture is in the form of platitudes. Their words are aspirational rather than based on reality.

Here are some common descriptions of company culture that, upon closer inspection, often fly in the face of reality:

"We are a highly collaborative culture." (Then why are star performers so often rewarded over team players?)

"We are a culture that rewards failure." (Then why are people so often berated when their ideas don't work out?)

"We're like a family." (Then you'd better be prepared to keep people on the payroll who do nothing or who do a terrible job.)

David Abbott once said, "I hate when people ask us about culture because it makes me feel like yogurt." But when you think about it, comparing business culture to yogurt isn't such a stretch.

In yogurt, it's the cultivation of the bacteria that ferments the milk that produces the yogurt's "culture." In a researcher's lab, other kinds of bacteria can be "cultured" in the artificial medium of a petri dish. But in organizational culture, the metaphorical bacteria are the codes of behavior that get cultivated in the working environment. The behavior produces the culture of the workplace and the company.

I've been privileged to be in the kitchen, so to speak, of many companies, which has enabled me to see deep inside their operations—where the yogurt gets cultivated. From this vantage point, I see what works and what doesn't. In the process I've developed some insights into how the culture at these companies works.

One of the things I've noticed is that organizational cultures vary more than most people think. And I've also come to realize that culture has more of an impact on business performance than you might imagine.

Will Guidara, author of *Unreasonable Hospitality*, is not afraid to proclaim, "'Cult' Is Short for 'Culture.'"[1] Many people, upon hearing that Guidara worked for the famed restaurateur Danny Meyer, would say, a little suspiciously, "Oh, you're working for the cult . . ." Eventually Guidara came to understand that "'cult' is what people who work for companies that haven't invested enough in their cultures tend to call the companies that have."

Guidara worked at a company whose owner gently pushed him to improve steadily every day, and where both his people and the customers were energized and refreshed by the experience of being there—they couldn't wait to come back. "The culture was strong, and it was working. Call it a cult!" Guidara wrote. "I was proud to be a part of it, and no amount of name-calling was going to convince me I was wrong."

MULTIPLIERS VS. DIMINISHERS

It's important to understand that organizational cultures are far more dependent on the person at the top than most people recognize. Even at a company like Procter & Gamble, which consistently hires and promotes from within, including the CEO, and where the company has a highly systematic approach to developing its people, that one person at the top still exerts a powerful influence.

The leadership consultant Liz Wiseman, a self-described "genius watcher," interviewed over 150 executives on their leadership styles. She also interviewed their current and former management teams.[2] Wiseman found that these leaders could be divided into what she calls diminishers and multipliers.

Some leaders, even if they were brilliant, managed to drain energy from others with their top-down, authoritarian style and their need to prove they were always right. As Wiseman wrote in her book *Multipliers*, "Other people's ideas suffocated and died in their presence and the flow of intelligence came to an abrupt halt around them." These were the diminishers.

The other category of leaders, the multipliers, used their intelligence to unlock and expand the creativity of their people. "When these leaders walked into a room, lightbulbs started switching on over people's heads."

Wiseman also found that there are a fair number of "accidental diminishers" within leadership ranks.[3] They started their careers with every intention of being multipliers but found themselves poisoned by the pervasive idea that they always had to be the smartest ones in the room. But self-awareness and intentional behavior changes can correct this, Wiseman asserts.

A big drawback of diminishers is that they consistently underutilize their people with their top-down, egocentric approach. Multipliers, on the other hand, know how to leverage the "intelligence and capability, enthusiasm and trust" of others, leading to an expansion of capacity that becomes greater than the mere sum of its parts (hence the word "multipliers").[4] Words that Wiseman came to associate with diminishers were "use," "blame," "tell," "decide," and "control." Words that motivated the multipliers included "develop," "explore," "challenge," "consult," and "support."

When a multiplier sits at the top of an organization, writes Wiseman, they see themselves not as a genius but as a genius maker. That's how they preside over the exponential changes—as opposed to incremental improvements—that are a sign of true creativity.

A CULTURAL CHECKLIST

To know how to nurture creativity within your organization, you need to make a conscious effort to codify your culture, focusing on the behavior that's encouraged and discouraged. This is something I realized I needed to do shortly after I became CEO of BBDO Worldwide.

A lot of us already knew intuitively what was working, so it wasn't as if the agency would fall apart if we didn't do this. But I was convinced that we could nurture and strengthen our culture if we actually spelled out its key elements.

So I brought together twenty people from around the world who I felt were doing the best work for the agency and asked them to come up with a list of behavioral qualities that they believed described BBDO's best people. I set aside half a day for the exercise because I thought that if I allowed three days, it would take three days. As it turned out, the group put the list together in a matter of forty minutes.

Here's the list of what defines our best people, of those who exemplify the culture of BBDO, according to the members of that group:

- They help make the work better.
- Their clients love them.
- They present well.
- They are hand-raisers, not finger-pointers.
- They're "we," not "me."
- They pick themselves up fast after being knocked down (everyone in this business gets knocked down).
- They are radiators, not drains (in terms of the energy they bring to a room).

- They are closers. (A fast "no" is way better than a slow "maybe.")
- They do the right thing.
- They have healthy paranoia.

Several years later, we added one more important quality:

- They actively seek out "different."

Our best leaders probably used these characteristics to evaluate people intuitively. But this exercise transformed the intuitive judgment of agency principals into a codified and sustaining network-wide set of principles.

I think every organization should perform this exercise. And it has to be based on and describe the reality of people's experiences rather than being a declaration of strategic intent.

If after doing this you decide you want to change your culture, then you can and you should. But you can't change it just by declaring what you want it to be. You change it by introducing new behavioral signals, because these mean so much more than words. And one of the most important signals of culture is what gets rewarded and what gets punished.

When GE introduced its "Imagination at Work" concept—which put a major emphasis on inventing new products and services—it made sure to include "imagination" as an attribute in performance reviews of the company's top 5,000 people. People had to provide evidence that they were taking a meaningful risk on a new project, that they were attempting to solve a problem in a new way, Beth Comstock, former chief marketing officer at GE, said in a recent interview.[5] "We had a series of metrics around it and progress reports."

Along with that, the company sought to make clear that when people were in experimental mode, they had permission to fail, she said. The idea of failure is scary for anyone, but it's especially the case if you're working for a company that is so focused on quality and precision, Beth said.

The leadership style of Jack Welch, Jeff Immelt's predecessor as CEO at the company, "made for a tremendous upside in terms of discipline and loyalty and stock price," Beth wrote in her book *Imagine It Forward*.[6] "Having 300,000 employees working in lockstep is powerful, but it's hard to enlist risky new ideas from people who are expected to do everything perfectly."

GE's Imagination Breakthroughs became "a protected class of ideas," Beth wrote in her book. They were "fully funded business bets that could not have their budgets cut because of a tight quarter, giving them space to take risks and grow into something valuable. We had to convince people that it was okay to have a failed idea, that this would not be held against them financially in a promotion review." It wasn't easy. "I told them this in no uncertain terms, but people had to believe it in their hearts. And their bosses and division CFO's often said otherwise. The tension could be thick."[7]

If, after an honest examination of your culture, you come to realize that you are rewarding the very qualities that stifle creativity, then yes, it is critical to take steps to change it. Not by demanding from on high that it must be done. Not by hiring some high-priced consultant to somehow make it happen. Cultural change has to come from deep within the organization.

When I lived in South Africa I attended Michaelhouse, a boarding school in KwaZulu-Natal. As a high schooler I was a vigorous anti-apartheid demonstrator. My best friend was named Andrew Redding, and I remember once going to Sunday lunch with him at his parents' house, which was near the school. Andrew's father, John, cooked the lunch, and I proceeded to thank him by getting into a horrific argument with him about politics. What upset me was that although he, like me, very much opposed apartheid, he also belonged to the very party that had implemented and institutionalized it: the Nationalist Party.

I behaved very much out of character that day in the late 1970s—I proceeded to rant at him, saying that he was a hypocrite. "How can you look at yourself in the mirror?" I asked him. And he looked at me and said, "You can lie in front of the trains protesting if you want. But the only organization in this country that has the power to change apartheid is the Nationalist Party. So if you really want to effect change, get inside the Nationalist Party and change it." With the passion of my teenage convictions, I refused to accept his argument.

Twelve years later, on February 11, 1990, I was driving over Hammersmith Bridge in London on my way to work listening to John Humphrys on BBC Radio 4. He was saying that Nelson Mandela had been released from prison, and that standing beside him was F. W. de Klerk, the president of South Africa and leader of the Nationalist Party. With tears streaming down my face I remembered that set-to I'd had with John Redding and thought, "Oh my god, he was right all those years ago. To change a culture, you need to work on it from within."

How do you change an organization's culture from within? One way is with a new shared language. Jeff Immelt realized how important that was when he introduced "Imagination at Work" at GE. Those three words were a signal to customers, investors, the public—and crucially, to GE's 300,000 employees—that a big change was under way.

"When you're the CEO of a company, frequently you're like a translator," Jeff said recently.[8] It wouldn't have been all that effective to tell the engineers to just go ahead and be creative. "You don't want your jet engine to be creative," he said. "It wasn't a word that was in our nomenclature, really. But the notion of trying new things, solving problems—those all go back to Edison. What I always did was use the words that meant creativity in the eyes of people who were working the businesses."

In the service of this objective, we at BBDO helped GE come up with an "equation" of words that would help express the new direction of the company. Part of it went as follows:

GE people = (unceasing curiosity + relentless drive + IMAGINATION) / risk x sweat^2 → breakthrough ideas

Cultural language will vary according to the industry. In *Unreasonable Hospitality*, Will Guidara recalls that Danny Meyer used language as a cultural signifier. In emails and meetings, he repeated key phrases that were central to his beliefs regarding hospitality, and he emphasized the "why" of these words over the "what," Guidara writes. Things like "constant, gentle pressure," Danny's version of the Japanese phrase *kaizen*, the idea that everyone in the organization should always be improving, getting a little better all the time. And another one: "Athletic hospitality," which translated to "always looking for a win, whether you were playing offense (making an already great experience even better) or defense (apologizing for and fixing an error)."

What does the cultural language of your organization say about your expectations? Remember that with the right cultural conditions and the right language, ordinary people can accomplish extraordinary things.

IT'S NOT ONE OR THE OTHER

An insight that many experts on business creativity miss is that the organizational characteristics that can kill ideas can be vital for the company's day-to-day operation. We want Boeing, Chase Bank, and Pfizer to be careful, methodical, and risk-averse when testing their products. Yet we also want the same companies to remove their blinders when envisioning the potential of next-generation technology in aviation, banking, and pharmaceuticals.

If you really understand your culture, you can find a way to inject creativity into it. We found this to be true at The Home Depot, which has more than 2,000 stores along with a healthy online business. It sells more than 1 million different products, and the way it stocks them changes depending on whether a store is in Bend, Oregon; Peoria, Illinois; El Paso, Texas; or Bangor, Maine. Customers in Atlanta are going to need different kinds of products than customers in Boston, and those products will change depending on the season. Lob in a couple of hurricanes or snowstorms and you have a whole new retail calculus to consider on short notice.

Just getting all those products onto the shelves is a staggeringly complex operation. For that reason, The Home Depot is serious about its operational efficiency.

When we got the Home Depot advertising account, one of the first things they told us was, "We don't do humor." And we got that. This was a company that had a clear understanding of who they were and what they did.

Then, against their express wishes, we went ahead and showed them a script for a humorous ad to run during the holidays. And guess what? They loved it, and we went ahead.

Why? Because it leveraged another truth rooted in their culture.

The Home Depot is justifiably proud of the 500,000 associates it employs—so much so that they draw about 90 percent of their leadership from that group. This is a company that doesn't have a headquarters. Rather, it operates a store support center to assist all the associates in all the stores. The executives are known to wear the same orange aprons as the associates on important company occasions to signal how important those jobs are to the company.

In the commercial, we locate the Home Depot store that is closest to the North Pole, in Fairbanks, Alaska. An announcer in a deadpan voice tries to find out whether Santa shops at that store. But all the associates in the store are fiercely protective of Santa's privacy, even as they are seen doing things like hauling huge bags of reindeer feed.

When asked whether Santa is a customer, one by one the orange-aproned Home Depot associates dodge the question.

"No comment."

"I can't comment on that."

"I don't know anyone by that name."

"Is he a contractor?"

"I can neither confirm nor deny that rumor."

"We didn't get an answer to that Santa question," the announcer concludes. "But we sure met some people who know a thing or two about giving."

This was an example of making a Creative Shift, toward humor, because we understood how The Home Depot worked and what was important to company executives. We showed them how humor could be used effectively as an homage to the associates—and it worked. If we had simply presented the idea without doing the initial groundwork, I don't think that ad would have come to fruition.

Because The Home Depot's leaders had such strong self-awareness about the company's culture—and because we respected that—we were able to give them a big creative nudge.

We had a similar experience with AT&T. We had generally emphasized the company's technological excellence in ads by showcasing the size and strength of its network, along with its lower fees, through the use of impressive statistics, charts, graphs, and coverage maps. The problem? Its competitors were doing that too. So we suggested something completely different for the NCAA Basketball Tournament, which AT&T was sponsoring: Have six-year-olds be the stars of the ads.

In encouraging people to participate in "Brackets by Six-Year-Olds," AT&T noted that, after all, "It's the people who know the least who create the best bracket." In one commercial, a boy told an adult interviewer that the San Diego State Aztecs would win because "their shorts are very comfortable." Another boy laid odds on the Florida Gators, because, he said, "I like dinosaurs."

The commercials were a breath of fresh air. And because the idea had clearly worked so well in this specific case, the company was able to stretch its boundaries and have six-year-olds humorously make the case for AT&T in other commercials as well. The theme? "It's not complicated." It was a risk that paid off, because it started small and executives could see that the concept was working before we expanded it.

GETTING EARLY BUY-IN

In order to achieve a Creative Shift, you need to identify those who make up the "artisanal class" within your organization and make sure they are on board with your plans as early as possible, Kellyn Smith Kenny, chief marketing and growth officer for AT&T, said recently.[9]

These are the people who are the most celebrated and revered—and the most powerful—within the organization. In effect, they shape the entire company's culture.

And these people will differ according to the type of organization. At AT&T, the artisanal class consists primarily of the people who work in finance and operations, Kellyn said.

Kellyn has worked in the past for Microsoft, Uber, and Hilton. At Microsoft (when she was there), the artisanal class consisted of engineers and enterprise sales, she said, and now it's moving more toward the product teams. At Uber, the artisanal people were mainly in product and sales. And at Hilton, they were largely on the business development and real estate teams.

It's critical for top management to establish "operational empathy" with the artisanal class, Kellyn said, along with other departments as well.

It's easy for marketers at a big company to think that the people in the artisanal class just don't understand marketing. Well, Kellyn countered, do those same marketers understand what a typical day is like for a financial analyst, or an engineer, or a product manager? Do the marketers understand what scares and motivates those people?

"If you are not in sync with the artisanal class, if you are recommending things that are antithetical to how they orient, it is like fighting gravity," Kellyn said.

Will there be conflict in the early stages of suggesting a big new idea? Of course. In fact, if you can actually bring healthy conflict to the surface in the beginning, so that everyone has a chance to contribute their varying opinions and ideas, "you are going to be in much better shape not just for buy-in, but the quality of what you execute will be far better because you were expansive in your problem-solving from the beginning," Kellyn said.

You can't just come up with a marketing message and be done with it, she said. "We have to make it true. Which means the product teams need to rework products, or the operations team needs to service customers differently. The finance team needs to budget for it. The lawyers need to be plainspoken on terms and conditions." And so on.

Of marketers, she said, "We're the storytellers, not necessarily the story makers."

"If what I'm saying isn't culturally ingrained in the company then it's just empty calories," she said. "Then I've just spent a lot of money saying something that our customers don't experience."

AT&T asked us to do something really big, and really different, when it was seeking to increase awareness of its small business services. Turns out people were very aware of AT&T's reach among consumers and big businesses, but smaller businesses were less likely to sign on with the company.

Our big idea? Reunite some of the actors from *The Office* to start their own business. Most ads targeting small businesses feature highly competent and organized people running bike shops, cheese shops, bakeries, etc. Instead, why not have people who are famously terrible at running a business start a business, and show how AT&T can help even them?

In the 2024 campaign, Rainn Wilson (who played Dwight Schrute on the show) develops a business idea that will "change the world": a pillow with speakers on either side featuring his voice, which is guaranteed to put you to sleep. "Just connect your phone to the pillow and enter dreamland," says Wilson in a hypnotic voice. "Because you can't dream if you can't sleep."

He convinces five of his former costars from *The Office* to join him in the start-up. (The company even faked a launch on LinkedIn and made some actual pillows.) As you might expect, their office is incredibly chaotic, and the coworkers are constantly sniping at each other. Fortunately, whenever technical difficulties arise, AT&T is able to fix the problem.

Getting six actors from the TV show together for a campaign represented a significant portion of AT&T's marketing budget. It was definitely risky. Kellyn knew it was key to get early buy-in and feedback from AT&T's artisanal class: mainly, the finance and operations people.

The campaign was enormously successful. Not only did it show that AT&T was working hard for small businesses, "but it also had a wonderful halo effect among big companies and consumers, because everyone loved these characters," Kellyn said.

A winning culture isn't always, or even mostly, a creative one. And that's okay. To reap the rewards of new ideas, most companies may not actually need to change the culture. The Home Depot and AT&T are cases in point.

But operationally focused companies need to approach creativity in an entirely different way than any other function.

As Peter Drucker said, "Culture eats strategy for breakfast." Culture is persistent and pervasive. If the organization's incentives reward a risk-averse mentality, you need to include a space that also rewards the Creative Shift.

THE RIGHT KIND OF FEAR

Organizational cultures can vary widely. But most experts agree on this: They should foster an atmosphere of psychological safety.

Harvard professor Amy Edmondson defines psychological safety as "the belief that the environment is safe for interpersonal risk-taking." In the workplace, this means that employees know that their contributions "are both *welcomed* and *expected*."[10]

When they're feeling psychologically unsafe, people are much less likely to speak up than when they feel safe and supported, and this can wreak havoc on both the operational side and the creative side of a company's work. Operationally, it can prevent people from pointing out potentially life-threatening errors in places like hospitals and manufacturing plants. On the creative side, the fear of being judged or punished prevents people from suggesting new ideas. It's scary to think of all the ideas that organizations have lost because they have instilled—whether consciously or not—this fear.

A workplace where psychological safety is a priority moves closer to becoming what Professor Edmondson called a fearless organization, "in which people feel truly engaged, inspired and willing to take the interpersonal risks of speaking up and experimenting that are necessary, so as to gain the shared rewards of making a difference—of creating great products and services that help customers and change the world in some small way for the better. In such organizations, people share a sense of what is at stake, why it matters—and why every one of us is needed to make progress."

Unfortunately, there are exceptions to this, and they simply can't be ignored. Two of the most creative entrepreneurs of our time—Steve Jobs and Elon Musk—managed to achieve great things by instilling a culture of fear in their organizations.

"Musk let loose a bitter laugh when he heard the phrase 'psychological safety,'" Walter Isaacson reports in his biography of Musk.[11] "His preferred buzzword was 'hardcore.' Discomfort, he believed, was a good thing. It was a weapon against the scourge of complacency. Vacations, flower-smelling, work-life balance, and days of 'mental rest' were not his thing."

"When things were most dire, he got energized," according to Isaacson. "But when he was not in survival-or-die mode, he felt unsettled. What should have been the good times were unnerving for him. It prompted him to launch surges, stir up dramas, throw himself into battles he could have bypassed, and bite off new endeavors."[12]

"A maniacal sense of urgency" is Musk's operating principle, says Isaacson—and he was able to harness that at SpaceX, Tesla, and Neuralink to goad his people to do things they didn't believe they were capable of doing. The results were decidedly less impressive at Twitter (now X), which he bought in 2022, and where people had been accustomed to a much kinder culture. Some people adjusted and embraced the new hardcore culture. For others (those who weren't laid off), it led to their resignations, which Musk was happy to accept.

A few times, Isaacson personally witnessed Musk reaming out an employee for what he saw as substandard work. When Isaacson later asked Musk whether it had been necessary to be so brutal to one employee in particular, Musk did not appear to recall the exchange.[13]

Like many people who worked with Musk, Michael Marks, an interim CEO at Tesla, found the experience to be trying in the extreme.[14] As he told Isaacson about Musk, "I've come to put him in the same category as Steve Jobs, which is that some people are just assholes but they accomplish so much that I just have to sit back and say, 'That seems to be a package.'"

Isaacson asked Marks, "Does that . . . excuse Musk's behavior?"

"Maybe if the price the world pays for this kind of accomplishment is a real asshole doing it, well, it's probably a price worth paying. That's how I've come to think about it, anyway." Then Marks added, "But I wouldn't want to be that way."

Like Musk, Jobs "was a brilliant but abrasive taskmaster with a reality-distortion field who could drive his employees crazy but also drive them to do things they thought were impossible," Isaacson wrote.[15]

I think Jobs was able to make fear work for him because he was both extraordinarily inspirational and unbelievably hardworking and demanding. The same is true for Musk. But Musk and Jobs are extreme rarities. Most leaders are not possessed of that level of visionary genius.

The dangers of a fear-based, top-down leadership style are well expressed in a FedEx TV commercial we did. An older executive in a well-tailored suit sits at the head of a table in the corporate meeting and says, "We have got to cut costs, people. Ideas?" A much younger, less nattily dressed worker hesitantly looks around the room and says, "We could open an account on Fedex.com and save 10 percent on online express shipping," followed by an insecure shrug.

His colleagues meet the idea with silence and skepticism until the executive slices his hands through the air and says, "Okay, how about this? We open an account on Fedex.com and save 10 percent on online express shipping." Suddenly everyone in the room *loves* the idea.

The late Phil Dusenberry, a longtime creative leader at BBDO, had his own quiet way of instilling what might be called a culture of fear—but in a positive way.

Phil was behind some of the most successful ad campaigns of all time, including "It's Everywhere You Want to Be" for Visa; "We Bring Good Things to Life" for GE; and the "Choice for a New Generation" Pepsi ads (including the one where Michael Jackson's hair accidentally catches on fire).

Phil was obsessed with craft and excellence. Nothing was ever really finished; it could always be better. He would keep pushing and pushing until there was simply no more time. In that respect, he was very much like the producer Lorne Michaels, who is known for saying about *Saturday Night Live*, "The show doesn't go on because it's ready. It goes on because it's 11:30."[16]

Phil had a very quiet voice. He sounded kind of like a radio deejay on the midnight to 2 a.m. slot. If you presented your work to him and it wasn't up to his standards, he would say, in that extremely quiet voice, "Is that all you've got?" Somehow his delivery was so much more deadly than if he had ranted and raged. No one wanted to be on the receiving end of that question. They dug deep and strove to present their best ideas because they were so determined not to disappoint Phil.

David Abbott was a much gentler leader than Phil, but you still hated the prospect of disappointing him. If you showed him work that he judged to be substandard, he would say, "I've seen your work, and I know you can do better." Quite an effective way of getting the best out of someone: *You* are good enough, but this particular example from you is not.

Both Phil and David were demanding without being demeaning; I would categorize both of them as multipliers. In her study of this style of leadership, Liz Wiseman, the business consultant and author of *Multipliers*, found that most multipliers possess a "hard edge." In other words, "they expect great things from people and drive them to achieve extraordinary results."[17] One person who worked for a multiplier described the experience as "exhausting" but also "exhilarating."

Sometimes, too, a culture of fear that emerges in the form of a burning platform—the sense of, "If you don't do something creative soon, you're going to die"—can force a company into being more creative.

Just look at Avon. The pandemic hit when James Thompson was a marketing executive at the non-US portion of the company. This was a company that hadn't changed much from its longtime model of selling beauty products door to door and in people's homes—pretty much a no-go once COVID-19 hit. Yes, Avon had a web presence, but it certainly wasn't at the forefront of online marketing; it was still relying pretty heavily on paper brochures.

The pandemic put fear in the hearts of Avon's leaders, and it also gave them an opportunity to rethink their whole approach. The Western European division of Avon really stepped up to digitize its marketing operations in a short time. And another department made extensive use of WhatsApp to connect with customers. In response to COVID, the company started making hand sanitizers, too. As James put it, "It was an amazing use of adversity."[18]

STORYTELLING FOR SOLDIERS

And now I'm going to talk about the US military. If that isn't a shift, I don't know what is.

A few decades ago, the military was beginning to realize that a too-strict culture was breeding paralyzing fear, along with conformist thinking and groupthink, among its soldiers.

This is a culture that operates, in most realms, under strict hierarchies and clearly defined rules. And yet the military has come to recognize that soldiers must also be trained to think outside the box, so that they know how to face situations where they must act beyond the scope of their commander's orders. Knowing when and how to do so requires deeply creative thinking.

In an article for a military journal, Milan Vego, professor of operations in the Joint Military Operations Department at the Naval War College, asserts that the authoritarian and bureaucratized nature of the military presents serious obstacles to creativity.[19] Among other things, he says, military commanders often make these mistakes:

Lead from the top-down, not the bottom up, and "yet in practice, it is from the bottom that creative ideas are usually generated."

Refuse to admit or learn from their mistakes, seeking to preserve an aura of infallibility.

Expect soldiers to blindly follow rules, regulations, and military dogma. This at the expense of critical thinking, experience-based knowledge, and a sense of mission.

Rely too heavily on lengthy, standardized lists.

Use opaque jargon and buzzwords, which "can be intended to impress the audience or readers, win arguments, or grossly inflate the importance of *un*important ideas."

Cultivate a parochialism that prevents cooperation among the various armed forces, reducing the likelihood that creativity will emerge during joint missions.

All of these qualities encourage a culture of conformity. And yes, "the military needs the stability of conformity so it can successfully function in peacetime and in war," Vego writes. "Yet at the same time it also has a paramount need for creativity; otherwise, it is doomed to failure when a supreme test of war comes. One of the most demanding tests for any military leader is to appropriately reconcile these contradictory requirements. Experience shows that military organizations that succumb to conformity eventually decline."

It's a credit to the US Army that a few years ago it hired a former neuroscientist and current English professor at the Ohio State University, Angus Fletcher, to encourage its officers to demonstrate creativity. At the Army's request, Professor Fletcher wrote a field guide for solders called *Creative Thinking*. The point of learning how to think creatively, he told his readers, was so that "even when you're surprised, you're prepared. Even in chaos, you advance with purpose. Even in calamity, you win."[20]

Fletcher's research focuses on how creativity works in the brain. Initially he was surprised when the Army approached him. As he told the Ohio State News Service, "I had a series of stereotypes about the Army—the Army's about order and discipline."[21] And the Army, he said, told him, essentially, "We need to empower our individual soldiers to be able to function when the plan breaks down. Basically, how do you come up with a second plan, what do you do if your first plan breaks? How do you create that next plan?"

"In the military you have to achieve your objective," Fletcher said in a separate interview for this book.[22] "And achieving your objective is different from following an order."

It's generally true that in the military you can follow an existing plan, Fletcher noted. A command is a plan that's been proven to be so effective over time that it becomes standard operating procedure. Soldiers need to use their common sense to determine whether a situation calls for following standard operating procedure or for shifting into creative mode with a brand new plan.

Fletcher made the case that coming up with creative solutions results in qualities that are also associated with what the military values—things like resilience, bravery, and adaptability. Using the power of narrative storytelling, he showed how sometimes military leaders have had to break the rules in order to save lives and achieve their mission.

For example, in 52 BC, Julius Caesar's Roman legion managed to overpower a Gallic army that outnumbered his by a factor of ten to one. How did he do it? By enlisting his soldiers to sneakily build first one circular ten-mile wall, and then another one, around Alesia, a major Gallic town and military stronghold—in just a few weeks. This trapped the Gallic fighters inside their own town and prevented them from exercising their superior military might over the Romans. But it broke the most basic rules of combat. The Gauls had been certain that Caesar would be forced to flee; instead, he used creative thinking to come up with a solution that had never been tried before.

A key element of creativity—in whatever realm—is surprise, Fletcher said. In the military, one of the most effective strategies is to surprise the enemy. His aim was to help soldiers develop new plans and new actions that bring about intentional surprise and thereby put the enemy at a disadvantage.

Another word for a plan is a "plot," or a "narrative." Fletcher, who has also worked with businesses including Pixar, said that these methods of setting up surprising and effective narratives essentially worked the same way in Hollywood when studios are developing new ideas for screenplays. And what is true for the military and for the movies, he said, also works in marketing.

Through various exercises, along with examples from military history, his field guide encourages Army officers to use their creativity in the most dangerous and unpredictable situations on Earth—when the "fog and friction" of war demands sudden action with very little information, and when the information that is available can be confusing. He sets out exercises that allow the flourishing of creativity in these types of situations while respecting—and harnessing—some of the key values of military culture.

The smartest minds in the military have long understood that creativity has an exponential impact. Soldiers who are well versed in creative thinking can pass that ability on to others. Organizations can apply this principle to their own cultures, Fletcher said. You can train one person on your team to be creative, that person in turn trains the rest of the team, "and that multiplies."

Creative military thinking exists off the battlefield, too. I'm sure it's no coincidence that the schools the Defense Department operates for the military are some of the best-performing schools in the country when it comes to test scores.[23]

What makes the difference? Among other things, it's that the schools benefit from the centralized structure of the military, which can implement creative solutions fairly uniformly at schools all over the country and the world. Compare that to public schools, where the actions of decentralized boards and governmental bodies can determine how well—or badly—a school district performs.

If one of the most compliance-based cultures on the planet can make the Creative Shift, then so can you. In the following chapter I'll demonstrate one key, and counterintuitive, aspect of achieving a creative transformation: the importance of being wrong at the right time.

CHAPTER 4

DO IT THE WRONG WAY FIRST. A LOT.

Before you can be good, you have to be bad. This is a key pillar of the Creative Shift.

David Guerrero, creative chair for BBDO in the Philippines, understands that you have to wade through a lot of crap before you get to the good stuff. He had this in mind when he was in Sri Lanka for work and went on a day trip to an elephant orphanage. After oohing and aahing at the cute elephants, he stopped at the orphanage gift shop and saw shelves of notebooks that, he was surprised to learn, were made out of elephant crap.

Elephants are vegetarians. Their diets consist mainly of grass, and so their poo is surprisingly fibrous and non-smelly, which makes it a good material to recycle into paper. And the typical elephant, as it turns out, produces loads of crap—up to 220 pounds of it—every single day. It typically defecates more than a dozen times a day, to the tune of 40 tons of dung per year.

What a perfect metaphor, Guerrero thought. And so he bought a load of the elephant-poo paper and took it back with him to Manila. (Customs officials asked him what it was and were a bit skeptical when he told them it was crap, but they ended up waving him through.)

Then he used the paper to publish *The Crap Ideas Book*, which shows how people need to generate a lot of crappy ideas in order to get to a few really good ones.

To a certain extent, creativity is about simple math. If you assume (as I do) that about 90 percent of all ideas are crap, then you need to come up with ten ideas before you know that you've found a single good one. Need ten good ideas? Then you'll need to throw out one hundred ideas to reach that number. Quantity leads to quality.

You shouldn't be generating ideas and then immediately killing them, Guerrero said in an interview.[1] "You have to separate the generative part from the judgment part."

While most of your business should focus on doing things the right way, the Creative Shift requires a different modus operandi.

Business as usual leads to the usual results. That's great if "the usual" involves landing planes on schedule, or manufacturing defect-free baby formula. If "the usual" no longer works because your products are rapidly becoming obsolete, think about the problem in the "wrong" way instead and see what happens. What do you have to lose?

I like to think that our WorkOuts produce a wealth of vigorous ideas, some to be discarded, some to be used now, and others to be used somewhere down the road, in as yet unknown ways.

Nurturing creativity means giving people freedom to fail, and really meaning it. When James Thompson was a marketing executive at Diageo, he sent a signal that it was okay to fail by starting a new feature at monthly town hall meetings: People, including himself, would talk about all the things they had done wrong. The "Here's how I failed" portion of the meetings became a big hit.

When Jeff Immelt was at GE, whenever something went wrong, he would make sure to stress "What have we learned from this?" over punishing people for their mistakes. And at Meta, engineers in testing mode regard crashing the system as a badge of honor, because it means they've tested something to an extreme and they can learn from the experience. Not only does this environment improve quality control, it also helps many more ideas rise to the surface—lots of bad ideas *and* a few really good ones.

Creativity needs to be one of the top two or three things that you validate and reward, James said: Reward people for nurturing ideas rather than discarding them, and for giving an idea the right amount of time to breathe instead of closing it down—regardless of whether the idea is eventually executed or successful.

BEGIN WITH THE ANSWER

If you accept the premise that creativity is a process that allows you to find totally new solutions to new or old problems, then you need the freedom to make an imaginative leap. You need to jump to conclusions without worrying about how you cross the intervening gap. Instead of inching your way, step by step, from data to solution in a logical progression, it's best to generate a chaotic array of possibilities and test them out on the problem until something clicks.

Sometimes people are able to use cause-and-effect reasoning to make a creative breakthrough. But I believe this is more the exception than the rule. Certainly, logical thought can be a big help when you're trying to make an improvement. But an improvement—which so many people call an "innovation" (essentially rendering that word meaningless)—is a far cry from a creative leap.

If more companies realized how critical it is to begin with the answer to an extremely well-thought-out question, they could start building up the muscle they need to come up with creative solutions on demand.

We tried this "begin-with-the-answer" approach when we were pitching for Johnson & Johnson's baby business. There were loads of people in attendance, from both J&J and

BBDO, who were expecting to hear a pitch that lasted two to three hours. Typically in pitching a campaign we would first talk about the brief (the instructions from the client), then do an analysis of the business situation, talk through the research that had been done in the area, and then make a strategic recommendation followed by a creative recommendation. And then we'd explain how our plan would play out in all the countries where the company planned to run the ads, and at the end we'd say, "Here are all of the reasons you should pick us."

The day before the J&J presentation I decided to completely flip the pitch around, which amounted to a big risk—a risk that was so big and scary, yes, but also so exciting, that my partner David Lubars and I each did a vodka shot and said cheers before meeting the audience.

Then I announced to the room, "Okay, I want everybody to close their eyes." After an initial jolt of surprise and suspicion, everyone closed their eyes, and we proceeded to play a sixty-second audio track of babies gurgling. That was it: just baby sounds.

When the gurgling stopped, I said, "You can open your eyes now." After explaining that the audio track had included recordings of babies from all over the world (speaking one universal language—baby), I said, "That's our idea: Nobody speaks baby like Johnson & Johnson. If you don't like it, we can just stop now. If you like it enough to continue, we'll go on and explain our plans for the campaign."

It was frightening to give the client the option to walk away after just a few minutes, but the risk paid off.

J&J listened to the rest of the pitch—and they gave us the business.

This approach was in full force when we came up with another theme—"You're not you when you're hungry"—for a Snickers campaign. It's one of the most successful campaigns in advertising history.

In the famous Super Bowl ad that kicked it all off in 2010, the legendary Betty White is shown in a pastel pantsuit, feebly playing football on a muddy field. After she gets pushed into a puddle, one of her teammates says, "Mike, what's your deal? You've been playing like Betty White out there." Betty gets angrier and angrier until someone thinks to give her a Snickers bar and she magically transforms back into Mike, a hardy football player who can keep up with the team again.

Cue the announcer: "You're Not You When You're Hungry. Snickers Satisfies."

Hilarious. And brilliant. (And incidentally, it pretty much single-handedly revived Betty White's post–*Golden Girls* career.)

To this day, clients ask how we got to the "You're not you when you're hungry" idea, as if it had been the first step in the creation of the campaign. They want to know what market research led us to the insight, then the foundational idea, and finally the Betty White script and campaign that drove millions to eat more candy bars. People always assume it was an act of brand-purpose-oriented, data-driven, logical deduction: When you're hungry, of course you act irrationally.

They can imagine the report that says, "Focus groups suggest that the hunger-reducing properties of Snickers candy bars are one of the reasons . . ."

But we certainly did not arrive at that insight fully formed. No, first we *stumbled* onto the idea and then we *caught* it. That line was buried in an otherwise mediocre script for Snickers. David Lubars spotted it and, in a creative leap, decided to build a campaign around it.

The Snickers bar has remained very much the same since it was first manufactured in Chicago in 1930. It's a combination of caramel, peanuts, and nougat in a coating of chocolate. It was meant to be a very filling snack bar when you were hungry, and it still is.

But a few years into the turn of the twenty-first century, that enduring truth had started to become rather humdrum, and Snickers had fallen to No. 7 in the chocolate category. The challenge became: How do you make something new and fresh out of the same old thing? A line like "Hungry? Eat a Snickers" just isn't going to cut it.

BBDO, which already had other Mars candy accounts, at first came up with a campaign that was very narrowly focused on the "lad" demographic, as epitomized by magazines like *Maxim*, that was all the rage at the time. But Mars knew that was the wrong approach for a brand with the universal appeal of Snickers. It was so unhappy with those ads that it took away the Snickers business from BBDO and gave it to another agency. "And honestly, we deserved it," David recalled.

Snickers is "a horizontal rather than a vertical brand that appeals to your grandma, your sister, your dad, everybody," David said. "And we lost sight of that."

Then, inexplicably, that other agency also came up with a "young hungry dude" approach. At that point Mars wearily said, "Let's give BBDO another try."

"I was so grateful to get a second chance," David recalled. He promised Mars he would come up with a campaign that capitalized on the candy bar's iconic status.

The first new brief from Mars was to create a Super Bowl commercial. David gave the assignment to five teams of people, who got busy writing down all kinds of Super Bowl scripts. And buried deep inside one of those scripts—barely calling attention to itself at all—was the line "You're not you when you're hungry."

David said the hairs on the back of his neck stood up when he saw that line. He knew it was the "reductionist nugget" (or, in the case of Snickers, you might call it a nougat) that could form the basis for a successful campaign. It was, as he put it, an idea that "was so flexible and stretchy that it could go anywhere in the world it needed to go." But he had needed to generate that huge volume of ideas first before he could discover that one magical idea.

The Creative Shift—in the form of people getting together to suggest lots and lots of mostly bad ideas until a really good one rises to the surface—made it possible for David to see the implications of the line, share this insight with his colleagues, and get support to see where it might lead.

Since 2010, the "You're not you when you're hungry" concept has been executed in myriad forms, evolving for different contexts in eighty-three countries around the world. It's still going strong to this day—proof of its foundational strength.

In the United Kingdom, we got a list from Google of the most frequently misspelled words in the search bar, and we paid for those misspelled search words (they were quite inexpensive) so that when people typed them in, an ad for Snickers came up that said, "You don't think straight when you're hungry."

And in Australia, we put together a promotional program for the 7/11 chain of stores called "Hungerithm." In it, we arranged for the price of Snickers to go up and down based on the mood of the nation, as determined by gathering data from social media accounts for negative and positive language. So when the people of Australia became more "hangry," they could get a Snickers bar at a reduced price using a QR code. In the course of six weeks, the price of Snickers changed 200 times based on the mood of the nation. Sales increased by 67 percent.

On social media, people all over the world have put their own creative spins on the idea that you turn into someone you're not when you're hungry, and that Snickers can fix it.

I'm convinced this campaign never would have been so successful if we had simply asked a group of people in a room to use logical, step-by-step reasoning to come up with a few good ideas for the campaign.

The deductive approach to being creative can seem like a path to certainty. And whether consciously or not, most people are conditioned to pursue certainty. In the idea-generation stage, though, you need to embrace uncertainty and let go of the idea of being right.

THE NEED FOR A SPACE TO BE BAD

That's why it can be so hard for compliance-based companies to make the Creative Shift. When you're a company like Boeing, and a door panel on one of the planes you manufactured blows out in midair, then something definitely went wrong in the manufacturing of the plane. You need to understand who did the wrong thing and why, and work quickly to make sure it never happens again. Maybe heads will need to roll (which they did at Boeing).

Many people—and especially people who work at compliance-based companies—are so afraid of making a mistake that they shut down when it comes to suggesting ideas. If you feel like you're on a high wire, there's no room to deviate. What if I'm wrong? What if I look foolish in front of my boss and colleagues? Will I be blamed if the idea doesn't work? For most people, closing down and seeking certainty and security in that environment is a very natural instinct.

That's why when leaders need to shift to creative mode, they must set up a separate space for their people where it's clear that they are being invited to come up with as many bad ideas as they can in a short period of time. (And why writing a book about crap on pieces of crap is an especially creative idea.)

The problem is that when people think they need a creative new solution, they expect their people to come up with one good idea. And yet most of the time, we have found, nine out of ten ideas are simply not good.

In reality, it's much more efficient to demand bad ideas— lots of them. Yes, you heard right: Not only should you give your people permission to have bad ideas, you should actively tell them to *try* to have bad ideas.

The process of asking for bad ideas does two things: It generates a lot of ideas, which in itself is a good thing. And then it goes beyond that by saying it's okay to have bad ideas. That immediately starts people thinking in a more open-minded and imaginative way, because they're no longer constrained by the need to be right, or good, or brilliant.

There are two platitudes that I hear a lot when it comes to creativity. One is that a good idea can come from anyone. The other is that there are no bad ideas.

To be truly creative in a group, you need to flip these ideas around and perform a kind of verbal jiu jitsu. The reality is that:

1. Bad ideas can come from everyone.
2. You need to generate as many bad ideas as you can in a short period of time.

As a leader, it's important to completely change the way your people look at the idea-generation process and create a space where they're actually encouraged to have lots of bad ideas. If you *must* reward people for anything at this stage, reward them for having the most bad ideas.

EVERYONE GETS THE CREDIT

Also, when you're in the idea-generation stage, you need to let go of the idea of "mine."

The very principle of collaborative creativity should be that everybody can generate ideas, including (and especially) bad ones. When a group of people generates lots of bad ideas, and then a few really good ones emerge, it's the group that has generated them, not an individual. Then, when you end up with some good ideas at the end, the credit for those ideas goes to the group. That's because you never would have reached the good ideas without everybody generating all of the ideas that they did. You won't ever be able to exactly trace what was stimulated in somebody's mind by exposure to one of the bad ideas.

The way our WorkOuts are structured, the ideas are owned by the group as a whole rather than by an individual person. Everyone can feel proud that they were all present at the birth.

In an episode of *Mad Men*, Peggy Olson, the ambitious young copywriter at Sterling Cooper, doesn't understand this when she accuses her boss, Don Draper, of stealing one of her ideas for a floor-cleaner and then taking credit for it.

Don will have none of it. "Are you out of your mind?" he says. "You gave me twenty ideas and I picked out one of them that was a kernel that became that commercial."

"It was about a kid locked in a closet because his mother was waiting for the floor to dry, which was basically the whole commercial," Peggy protests.

No, Don says, because he was the one who made the idea workable. What were they going to do? Film the entire commercial in a dark closet?

"But you got the Clio," Peggy points out.

"It's your job!" Don says. "I give you money and you give me ideas."

Peggy is still mad, and rightly so. The truth is that *both* Peggy and Don played a role in producing a successful commercial. If Peggy hadn't had the idea, Don wouldn't have been able to recognize its potential and make it workable.

LET "CRAPGPT" GIVE YOU A HAND

Artificial intelligence is very good at coming up with loads and loads of ideas, and, unlike Peggy, it doesn't care about getting credit. It also doesn't care about looking stupid. David Guerrero notes that to some extent AI is even replacing humans on the idea-generation front. "AI is the elephant dung of the tech world," he asserted. One of his colleagues even considered calling it CrapGPT.

I actually think that ChatGPT or a similar chatbot should be included as a nonhuman participant in WorkOuts—not for the quality of the ideas, but because AI is so outstanding at generating lots of ideas quickly.

I don't think AI poses any kind of threat to real human creativity. Humans will always have the edge in coming up with completely new solutions. But I'm very excited by the ways AI is aiding humans in the *execution* of new ideas—especially in the visual realm.

Of the three seismic changes in my industry that took hold after I became CEO—the internet, the smartphone, and AI—I actually think AI is the most exciting, because of its potential to realize creative ideas, to bring them to life. Certainly in terms of creating content it is by far the most important.

At BBDO, AI is affecting every single part of our workflow. It's making it easier for us to analyze data. To synthesize information about audiences. To develop and test hypotheses. To optimize results. And in the process, it's eliminating a whole load of work.

The gap between having an idea and bringing it to life can be huge in terms of time, money, and technical possibility. And AI, particularly as it relates to video imagery, is allowing us to close all three of those gaps.

At BBDO, we can hypothetically say, "Wouldn't it be fantastic if a polar bear could skate around Rockefeller Center while drinking a can of Pepsi?" AI can then instantly show us a video of a skating polar bear, which we can further manipulate if we decide to move forward with the idea. No need to try and train a real polar bear to skate.

We recently did a commercial that featured a new and an old VW minivan. Driving the new minivan was a famous Brazilian singer, while her mother—also a famous Brazilian singer—drove the older one, with the two singing a song about generational change.

What made this commercial magical was that the mother had died almost twenty years earlier. Because of AI, we were able to bring the mother and daughter together on film.

Angus Fletcher, the Ohio State professor who has developed creativity exercises for the military, scoffs at the idea that AI could ever replace humans in generating breakthrough new ideas.

"A computer can tell you what worked yesterday and keep reproducing that," he said in an interview. That's why AI is never going to take over the world. It can only do things that it knows has worked in the past. "The bizarre paradox is that we think data is the source of intelligence, and we're investing all this money in something that is dumber than the thing we already have in our heads."[2]

In terms of sheer volume, AI is very useful at generating bad ideas. To which I say, more power to it.

I've seen it happen time and again. When you see bad ideas—and when you know they're bad—they organically act as a springboard to the good ideas. But you have to wade through all that badness first.

David Abbott said that when he first sat down to work on an ad, the first thing he did was write the worst headlines he could imagine. He needed to get those out of the way before the good ones would emerge.

"I jot down thoughts or phrases that come to mind before I need them," he wrote. "I also write down in the margins all the cliches and purple bits that clutter my head. I find that only by writing them down do I exorcise them. If I simply try to forget them they keep coming back like spots on a teenage chin."[3]

It's the same in groups. But it can also be harder in groups, unless the leader creates an environment where bad ideas are actually encouraged.

WINNOWING THE GOOD FROM THE BAD

After you have plenty of ideas, mostly bad ones, you need somebody who can catch the good ones and decide how best to use them. It's an entirely different phase of the process.

It's critical to embrace crappy ideas in the idea-generation stage, but this is *not* what you do in the execution phase.

Guerrero strongly suspects that a disastrous ad campaign for Philippine tourism ("It wasn't done by us," he stresses) was the result of logical, step-by-step thinking toward a single idea, and then executing that one idea—a process that almost never works.

Launched with great fanfare that included fireworks, the world campaign featured a tagline praising the beauty of the Philippines—*in Filipino*—a language that hardly anyone outside the Philippines knows. In addition, a prominent campaign logo was found to be almost identical to one used by Poland.

The whole country started making fun of the campaign on social media (I guess you could argue that was a kind of backhanded success), and it led to the resignation of the tourism secretary.

The new tourism secretary immediately called for ad agencies to submit their pitches, and BBDO won the account.

The original idea would have been perfectly fine in the idea-generation stage. In fact, "Hey, let's urge people to come to the Philippines in Filipino" might even have won an award in a bad-idea contest. The big mistake was to allow it to reach the execution stage.

The BBDO team in the Philippines proceeded to come up with lots of bad ideas for the tourism campaign. Guerrero and his team welcomed them enthusiastically.

And then, one day, Guerrero was on holiday in the Philippines, going scuba diving, and thinking what an incredibly enjoyable experience it was—a lot more fun than it would have been, say, in the North Sea in Britain. And that's when the foundational idea came to him: Everything is more fun in the Philippines. Diving, commuting, even climbing stairs—they're all more fun.

He was unable to write the idea down while underwater, but once he was back on land he quickly scribbled it onto a piece of paper. And from there it went to the execution stage.

Yes, he was the one who technically came up with the idea. But, he said, "I would never have got to that idea if it hadn't been for all the bad ideas that came before."

Almost immediately after the campaign launched, ordinary Filipino citizens started coming up with their own versions of the ads in memes, putting their own spin on the types of activities that make the Philippines such a fun, warm, and welcoming place. These included a few cheekier examples of the concept—things like "Corruption is more fun in the Philippines."

In all, over 70,000 memes were recorded. And the campaign picked up a Grand Prix for Asian Strategy from the World Advertising Council in 2013.

That was the ultimate sign of a creative foundational idea because it opened the door for numerous people to come up with their own version of it. And it was executed with great creativity.

While "having the idea" is seldom the result of one person sitting alone, at BBDO we can and do honor the people who execute something brilliantly, and nominate them for awards.

In an interview, Steve Jobs once said that people are prone to the "disease of thinking that a really great idea is 90 percent of the work. . . . And the problem with that is that there's just a tremendous amount of craftsmanship in between a great idea and a great product, and as you evolve that great idea it changes and grows."[4]

He added, "And you also find that there's tremendous trade-offs that you have to make. There are just certain things you can't make electrons do, there are certain things you can't make plastic do or glass do . . . or factories do or robots do. And as you get into all these things, designing a product is keeping 5,000 things in your brain . . . and continuing to push to fit them together in new and different ways to get what you want."

It's one skill to come up with ideas. It's another skill to catch the best ideas, and another one to shape the best idea into a final product. The catching and the execution are not something that should be done by a large group. These should be done by experts. And the craftspeople who create their own special magic around a great idea should definitely get credit for what they were able to accomplish when it achieves a high standard.

But those craftspeople also should recognize that they never would have gotten to that point without the tremendous power of unleashed group creativity. When you bring together people with very different backgrounds—some with lots of expertise in the area to be discussed and others with none—then the power of unlike notions, combined with bad ideas, works its magic.

The bad-idea generation sessions that we highlight in our WorkOuts—and that any company can adapt to its own culture—are a tribute to the power of collaborative, as opposed to individual, creativity.

Organizations are surprisingly capable of tapping into this creativity, no matter what industry they are in, and it's a waste of their collective talent if they don't.

5

HARNESS THE CREATIVE POWER OF YOUR PEOPLE

Clients often tell me, "We simply don't have the right people to come up with breakthrough ideas." They think that hiring "creative" people from elsewhere will solve their problems. This is nonsense.

I guarantee you: You already have the people you need to be more creative. You just need them to behave more like five-year-olds. And it wouldn't hurt to bring out the karaoke machine, too. (I'll explain why a bit later.)

Contrary to what many corporate leaders may think, a company's people are rarely why the company finds itself out of ideas. That's because nearly every human being has the capacity to make the Creative Shift. Your people are in the trenches, face to face with the problem. If they can't think of new things worth trying, some overpriced corporate consultant certainly won't.

In a typical move, a bank will hire a marketer from a company known for its creative marketing campaigns: "Company X is so good at thinking outside the box—we'll just hire their head of marketing to do that for us." Inevitably, the transplant is rejected by the host because (a) the new person doesn't know the industry and gets left behind by the leadership team, or (b) if they do catch up, being given the remit to "make things creative" without the authority and resources to follow through is pointless.

As a leader, you can create the conditions that enable your people to make the Creative Shift and apply their innate potential. Instead of blowing your budget on bringing in creative "stars," help your people be more creative and invest in testing their ideas instead. The key is to work with the talent you already have but aren't fully leveraging. In this way you become what the consultant Liz Wiseman calls a multiplier, rather than a diminisher, and you'll see changes that can be measured in orders of magnitude.

James Thompson, the former marketing executive I introduced earlier, recalled how one of his brand managers approached him just as James was ramping up efforts for Diageo to be more creative with its products and marketing. "We had just integrated five regional companies in America into one national one, and there wasn't a lot of growth at the time," James recalled recently.[1]

The man told him, "I think I'm probably not in the right place." James asked him why, and the man said, "Because I'm not creative. I'm good at a lot of things but not that."

James appreciated the man's honesty—he knew what was expected of him and genuinely believed he couldn't deliver on it. But James, who had worked with the man for about five years, knew otherwise: "I said, let's not have the argument about whether you're creative or not. Because I could argue that you are, and you could argue that you're not, and we'll be here until next week."

This person "was really good at running a tight ship," James recalled. He worked well with everybody—not that he would win a popularity contest, because he was quite tough-minded—but everyone respected him. He was outstanding at executing incremental improvements and getting the organization behind him on those improvements. "But he could only give us half of what we were asking for. Or so it seemed," said James.

James suggested that, regardless of how the man saw himself, he should position himself as having a reputation for valuing creativity and becoming a magnet for it—not only inside the company but also with clients and outside partners like ad agencies. "And I kept raising the bar. I kept saying, we can't just do more of the same-old same-old."

The man ended up moving into the innovation department, where he took James's advice and became known as a champion of creativity. One way he achieved this was by bringing together a team of diverse thinkers, including some people who might have come off as eccentric. One of these hires, James recalled, was an introverted, chain-smoking hippie type given to gnomic pronouncements who came up with brilliant insights and inspired other people on his team to come up with original ideas, too.

The man who claimed he wasn't creative gave his team members a space to be different and weird, and because of that they were extraordinarily successful and generally got the biggest bonuses of anyone, James said.

But they never would have been so successful without their boss's operational and political skills, which enabled the best ideas to receive backing from senior leadership. As James put it, "He could be more left-brained in the organization, which helped him get the right-brained things through."

One of the department's new products was a peach-flavored whiskey that was more than an incremental improvement. It transformed the market by changing the image of whiskey from that of a drink favored by aging men to something that both women and younger men wanted to drink. It was a "real change that ignited growth in the category again," James said.

"Creativity is not a talent," said the wildly creative comedian John Cleese in a speech he gave for Video Arts, a video production company that he cofounded. "It is a way of operating."[2]

Assuming you are above a certain level of intelligence, creativity is unrelated to IQ, Cleese said, citing research by the psychologist Donald MacKinnon, one of the pioneers of creativity research.

As MacKinnon noted in a 1964 paper, what creative people lack in "verbal intellectual giftedness," they make up for "with a high level of energy, a kind of cognitive flexibility which enables them to keep coming at a problem with a variety of techniques from a variety of angles; and being confident of their ultimate success they persevere until they arrive at a creative solution."[3]

Like so many other researchers after him, MacKinnon found that creativity *is* directly related to a person's ability to play.

In his speech, Cleese explained that people can function at work in two ways: open or closed. In the closed mode, "We have inside us a feeling that there's lots to be done and we have to get on with it if we're going to get through it all." Closed mode is highly purposeful and features tension, anxiety ("although the anxiety can be exciting and pleasurable"), and not much humor.

To fully achieve open mode and flourish within it you need confidence, humor, and a "space/time oasis," Cleese said. "You can't become playful and therefore creative if you're under your usual pressures, because to cope with them you've got to be in the closed mode. So you have to create some space for yourself away from those demands. And that means sealing yourself off. You must make a quiet space for yourself where you will be undisturbed."

And it means bringing a sense of play to your work.

WHEN LEGO LOST ITS WAY

Recently my colleagues from Omnicom Media Group were invited to pitch for the global media account of LEGO. These meetings tend to be very formal and serious, as hundreds of millions of dollars are often at stake. But in this case, when my colleagues showed up at the LEGO office in Boston, they were shown into a conference room where they were each given a bucket of LEGO bricks.

The clients said, "You've got twenty minutes. Build something."

My colleagues worked together to build a rocket, complete with a satellite that could be launched from it. They were able to make it part of their presentation as a metaphor for their ability to collect information, data, and signals, and for the way this informed their media planning.

It might be hard to imagine, but back in the mid-1990s LEGO itself lost sight of the power of play. The company was no longer at the top of its category. Its colorful interlocking bricks, introduced in 1958, were proving to be no match for products powered by trendy new technologies, such as the Nintendo GameBoy. Kjeld Kirk Kristiansen, the company's CEO and a grandchild of LEGO's founder, knew that something needed to be done to stimulate new creative energy within the company.

So in 1996, Johan Roos and Bart Victor, then professors at the International Institute for Management Development (IMD) in Switzerland, traveled to Denmark to lead strategy sessions with 300 LEGO managers at the company's world headquarters.

When they arrived, Roos and Victor observed that the managers all had big bowls of LEGO bricks on their desks, and yet he never saw them playing with the bricks. "Despite the playful aura around this family-owned company, in 1996 LEGO managers were not much different from managers anywhere. In their view, methods or materials that appeared playful, childish, or frivolous did not belong in serious business discussions," they recalled in a paper they wrote.[4]

Roos and Victor set about encouraging the managers to take a break from their spreadsheets, whiteboards, and flipcharts and actually play with the bricks their company manufactured.

"During these programs, we tasked managers to give their own subjective meaning to the great variety of colours, textures, shapes, and sizes of LEGO materials and use their hands to construct, deconstruct, and reconstruct that meaning, then develop and share stories about what they had built," Roos and Victor recalled in the paper.

He and Victor weren't exactly sure what the result would be. Victor had a background in early childhood education, but he didn't know whether playing with LEGOs would have a meaningful impact on adults.

The results, as it turned out, far exceeded the professors' expectations. The managers were surprised and impressed by "the emergence of new and surprising insights and how the playful constructions facilitated serious dialogue."

The experience at LEGO was so positive that Roos and Victor decided to pursue what they knew might be considered an "insane" idea: to work with LEGO to develop a program to help managers at other companies generate creative new business solutions. They collaborated with a LEGO designer to come up with the right materials and structures, and then tested them on managers attending the IMD school, along with a few skeptical but open-minded company executives.

The result was the LEGO Serious Play program, which is still going strong and has been used by companies as diverse as IKEA, Samsung, Virgin Atlantic, and Hitachi to help them develop new strategies, processes, and products.

The credo of LEGO Serious Play, according to its practitioners, is as follows:

- Leaders don't have all the answers.
- Your success depends on hearing all the voices inside the room.
- People naturally want to contribute, be part of something bigger, and take responsibility.
- Often teams work sub-optimally, leaving knowledge untapped in team members.
- We live in a world which best can be described as sophisticated and adaptable; allowing each member to contribute and disseminate results in more sustainable business.[5]

With the help of a trained facilitator, participants create LEGO models to address a particular challenge or answer a specific question, and then tell stories and share ideas about it. Proponents of the method say it encourages equal participation and discourages groupthink because individuals must create their own models and narratives as part of a larger shared landscape.

The program takes advantage of what's known as "hand knowledge." As two LEGO Serious Play facilitators noted in a guide on the method, "A surprisingly large part of the human brain is dedicated to controlling the hands. Therefore, when people construct things with their hands, they simultaneously construct theories and knowledge in their minds. When we 'think with our hands' we create more new neural connections thus unleashing creative energies, new modes of thought, and novel ways of seeing what most adults have forgotten they even possessed."[6]

The child psychologist Jean Piaget said that "play is the work of childhood." Bringing play into the workplace is one way to bring out the inner creative child that is hiding within us, waiting to be released.

THE CREATIVE COST OF ADULTHOOD

In the late 1960s, NASA wanted to identify who its most creative people were so it could assign them its hardest problems.[7] So they asked George Land, a renowned creativity researcher, to come up with a test that specifically measured imagination. The test proved to be quite accurate and predictive as far as engineers and scientists were concerned, but it didn't answer a basic question: Where does creativity come from? Are some people born with it, and others not? Is it something people can learn?

To find out, Land decided to give his creativity test to a representative sampling of five-year-olds (it was simple enough in its design that they could easily grasp the exercises). To Land's astonishment, 98 percent of the five-year-olds tested in the "creative genius" category as defined by the test.

The result was so unexpected that Land decided to turn the test into a longitudinal study. When he administered the test to the same group of children when they were ten years old, he found that a mere five more years of living and being educated had taken their toll: Only 30 percent of the children now showed up as creative geniuses. And by the time they were fifteen years old, the number had fallen to 12 percent.

And now for the most depressing result of all: A sampling of the group as adults showed that only 2 percent of them were now in the creative genius category.

What happened to all that imagination? Some of it was the inevitable result of neurobiology, but society stamped a lot of it out, too. And with good reason. A certain amount of conformity and compliance is needed for society—and organizations—to function.

There are two kinds of thinking that occur in the brain, according to Land: divergent and convergent. "One is like the accelerator and the other is like the brake," he said in a TedX Talk in 2011.

Divergent thinking is where you make new connections and develop new possibilities. Convergent thinking is where you evaluate and make judgments and criticize.

And convergent thinking usually wins, especially when you're a working adult. Convergent thinking is what causes someone to say, almost before someone has finished suggesting an idea, "That's crazy," "That doesn't fit our policy," "That will cost too much," and so on, Land said.

Only by thinking more like five-year-olds can we create a new future that solves the new problems that we have never seen before, he concluded. We all have that capability. We just have to find ways to unlock it.

Alison Gopnik, a psychology professor at the University of California at Berkeley, has also noted that maturity comes at a creative cost.

Compared with other animals and even other primates, humans have extremely long childhoods, followed by an extended adolescence, with their brains going through different phases of development.[8] "Young children have characteristic deficits in executive function, working memory, attentional focus, and control," Gopnik writes.

And according to Gopnik, "these are precisely the same abilities required for performing complex skilled actions swiftly and effectively in adulthood. Indeed, human children are so dependent on others partly because of their deficits in these areas." But what they lack in their ability to rent an apartment or hold down an office job they more than make up for in their capacity to come up with wildly imaginative ideas.

The brains of young children are very busy making synaptic connections, and as they get older, while some of these connections are strengthened, others are pruned for efficiency, "transforming a more flexible, sensitive, and plastic brain into a more effective and controlled one," Gopnik says.

Think about the effect of that on your creativity, if you can, with your pathetically fewer remaining synaptic connections.

Actually, if you had maintained all the synaptic connections you had when you were an infant, you'd never be able to get anything done, Angus Fletcher, the professor at Ohio State University quoted in Chapter 3, said in a recent interview.[9] Too many neurons would be firing across all the different pathways all at once.

The fact is, most adults are failing to activate many of the neural pathways that remain in their brains, until they simply go dormant. "You don't actually need new branches, you just need to activate the ones that you have," Fletcher said. That's what creative thinking does.

"Our neurons on an individual level are narrative machines," he noted, and when they connect with other neurons in new ways, they create new narrative pathways that can be harnessed to find new solutions.

Professor Fletcher's exercises have helped the military and other groups to regularly exercise their brains to develop creative plans in the face of unexpected situations. It's a kind of basic training in creativity.

These exercises train your brain to do what it naturally wants to do, he said. But nurturing creativity needs to become a practice and a habit because there is so much in society that is working against it.

Before Josy Paul started BBDO India for us in 2008, he headed up an agency called David that was part of the Ogilvy agency network and the WPP group. It was a time when more big brands from overseas were starting to realize the enormous potential of India. As Josy explained it in an interview, "The Goliaths were coming, so maybe the smaller agencies in India needed some support. So I set up David."[10]

He designed the office as a playschool, with furniture and carpets in bright primary colors and toys everywhere. "I wanted it to be the opposite of everything I had experienced in advertising," he said. Before you entered David, you had to sign a letter saying you had resigned from adulthood and were committed to summoning your inner child for a spirited play session.

I like to think our WorkOuts at BBDO are one way of doing that. It's a way to provide our people and our clients with a metaphorical sandbox to play in where "crazy" or "bad" or "silly" ideas are not just allowed, they're actively encouraged.

ENCOURAGING KARAOKE CONFIDENCE

Back in the late 1980s, when I was account director for Philips Consumer Electronics at Ogilvy, I was asked to do a self-evaluation prior to a job review. Asked about my greatest contributions that year, I wrote down that one of the biggest was convincing Philips *not* to introduce a karaoke machine into its line of products.

This was after Philips had launched LaserVision, a disc player that was a resounding flop. I was certain that I had prevented another big failure at the company. Have untrained singers belt out-of-tune songs into a microphone? I couldn't see the appeal. But of course, as I now see, I was dead wrong.

And that's because of one thing I failed to see back then: how karaoke generates confidence.

Tom Kelley and David Kelley, of the design company IDEO, encourage leaders to promote what they call "karaoke confidence" in the workplace. Most people would be terrified to get up on a stage and sing in front of an audience. But a karaoke stage is different.[11] There is no pressure to be good, and while the audience certainly appreciates singers with talent, they shower just as much—if not more—applause on someone who may not carry a tune very well but makes up for it with large doses of energy and enthusiasm.

The Kelley brothers realized that the same factors that cause lousy, shy, and inexperienced singers to get up on a stage and perform also exist in creative workplaces. In their book *Creative Confidence*, they offer five guidelines to cultivate more karaoke confidence in groups:

- Keep your sense of humor
- Build on the energy of others
- Minimize hierarchy
- Value team camaraderie and trust
- Defer judgment—at least temporarily

The first and most important step for leaders to take is to recognize that their people are creative and to communicate that they believe this is so. Too often, leaders leave this step out, or else they signal through their behavior that their people's ideas actually *don't* count. Certainly, hiring an outside consultant is a tacit, yet very powerful, signal that no one already employed by the company is believed to be good enough to solve a creative challenge.

IDEO has helped thousands of companies expand their people's creative capacity. As the Kelley brothers put it in the introduction to their book, "We have been stunned at how quickly people's imagination, curiosity, and courage are renewed with just a small amount of practice and encouragement." People who tap into their full creative potential, say the Kelleys, feel as if they've unknowingly been driving with their emergency brake on and have finally released it.

Referring to the work of Carol Dweck, a psychology professor at Stanford, the Kelleys discuss the importance of the "growth mindset," where people believe that no matter what their age or past experience, they are capable of charting new creative territory. The growth mindset is to be contrasted with its evil counterpart, the "fixed mindset," where people believe their abilities are innate and inflexible. A fixed mindset keeps people locked inside their comfort zones, too afraid to try new things for fear of revealing their supposed ignorance and creative unworthiness to others.

Making the Creative Shift at an organization requires a growth mindset, and it needs to start with the person at the top. Individual workers can cultivate this trait within themselves to positive effect, but the CEO of a company has more influence over culture than anyone else—and more than he or she probably even realizes. It's through their behavior, words, and practices that they will be able to persuade everyone else at the company that they have creative ideas to contribute.

I really have had leaders tell me, "I wish our people were more creative." But it's not that their people aren't creative—all people are born creative—it's that they haven't been given an effective channel to release their ideas.

Many executives fail to see the creative potential of their own people, Patricia Corsi, chief growth officer for Kimberly-Clark, said in an interview.[12] Patricia is a great believer in internal crowdsourcing that encourages *all* people to contribute ideas, and she has utilized it at all the companies where she has served as a marketing executive, including Bayer, Heineken, Unilever, and Kraft.

When Patricia was chief marketing officer for Heineken Mexico, she assigned a trainee to develop a "creative challenge of the month." Each month, the marketing department would put up posters in the cafeteria, meetings rooms, breakrooms, and so on announcing a very specific challenge. The ideas suggested would be winnowed down to three, and the people who had come up with them would present them, in the style of the *Shark Tank* reality show, to the marketing department. Prizes included things like a two-week trip to learn new skills at a company partner such as Twitter or Google.

One of the challenges was this: How do we extract the most value out of our sponsorships in baseball? At the time, Heineken seemed to be sponsoring every sport under the sun, and it was very expensive, Patricia recalled. Sometimes there's "a little too much testosterone" in the beer space, she said, and it started to feel like Heineken was sponsoring teams just because it wanted to block a competing brand from doing so.

After finding out about the challenge, one person in sales suggested an idea that came to be called "Catch a Million." Inspired by an effort he had heard about in Japan, he proposed that Heineken sell T-shirts with its logo on them and promise to give 1 million Mexican pesos (about $50,000) to anyone who caught a fly ball during a game while wearing one of the shirts.

Not only did a lot of people start wearing the shirts during games, providing additional advertising for Heineken, but the company made a not insignificant amount of money from sales of the shirts. Compared to how much Heineken was paying for the sponsorship, the money spent on Catch a Million was negligible, but the payoff was huge.

Another Heineken challenge: How do we make the music festivals we sponsor more sustainable? Anyone who has been to a music festival has seen all the plastic beer cups that pile up in garbage cans or end up strewn across the grounds. Seeing the nature of the challenge, someone from the procurement department did some research and discovered a way to manufacture cups out of some the residues from the ingredients used to make beer. The materials used for the cup were compostable like food.

Heineken adopted the idea, and ingredients that would have been discarded or fed to cattle were instead reused for the festival cups. The woman who came up with the idea won a global award for sustainability from Heineken.

HOW TO HANDLE YOUR STARS

Certainly, many companies employ people who are prolific generators of great ideas. Of course you don't want to hold those people back, but you also want to be aware of the signaling that goes on around these stars. You want to make clear to other employees that this is only one person who is capable of coming up with great ideas.

If you rely too heavily on these star players, then you signal to the rest of your workforce that they don't need to be creative, or that they aren't capable of being creative. And in the process, you will miss out on some truly inventive ideas that have been suppressed.

And there are different kinds of stars, too. An HR consultant I heard speak at a conference said leaders need to distinguish between their prima donnas and their MVPs. Shaquille O'Neal was an MVP, he said, whereas Kobe Bryant was a prima donna. Shaq achieved thirty-five points a game by making the whole team better, and Kobe was the guy who delivered thirty-five points on his own. You needed both on the team, but you needed to coach them very differently.

Sometimes it's worth it to employ creative prima donnas and accede to their self-important demands. As the HR consultant said, if they want a big office in the corner, give it to them, but not on the same floor as everyone else.

As they lavish rewards and attention on their outside consultants and their internal stars, many leaders miss the invaluable insights they could be getting from the people on the front line, including customer service agents, salespeople, line workers, and delivery workers. Their upfront operational knowledge can help them make a Creative Shift—provided they are in the right environment. The closer you are to the problem, the more likely you are to invent a completely new solution.

If you task only your most senior people and your stars with solving a creative challenge, then you're missing a trick. You need someone in the room who actually does the coding, or handles customer complaints, or puts together the parts on the assembly line, and so on. By involving them in creative discussions, you strongly signal how valuable they are to the culture, too.

Love him or hate him, Elon Musk gets this. In setting up his SpaceX factory, Musk "followed his philosophy that the design, engineering, and manufacturing teams would all be clustered together," Walter Isaacson writes in his biography of Musk.[13] The people working on the assembly line should be able to immediately locate a designer and ask why a particular part or machine was made a certain way, because they're the ones who see firsthand how it's working or not working, Musk explained.

As Musk put it, "If your hand is on a stove and it gets hot, you pull it right off, but if it's someone else's hand on the stove, it will take you longer to do something."

THE POWER OF UNLIKE NOTIONS

Abigail Posner, director of creative works at Google, gives speeches on creativity to organizations that have included accounting firms and electricity distribution companies.

Her message: All people are inherently creative. It's a quality that's not just the domain of artists and musicians and designers. Her goal is to decode the creative process so that, for example, at YouTube (which Google owns), engineers can collaborate to develop and leverage content that is entertaining and profound.

I first met Abigail when we were on a panel together at Cannes, and I was immediately impressed by her ability to keep asking questions as opposed to positing ideas. She keeps asking: Why? How? What's the connection? In that way she achieves insights, and arrives at solutions, that no one else has imagined.

Abigail believes in what she calls "the power of unlike notions." When these notions come together they have the potential to uncover something both novel and helpful. The combinations can manifest themselves at both an individual and an organizational level, and when you harness both levels together, they can have an exponential impact.

She recently gave a monumental example of this: the reversal of damage to the ozone layer, which protects the Earth from dangerous ultraviolet radiation.[14] In the 1980s, scientists began warning that certain industrial chemicals were depleting the ozone layer and threatening the environment. It was a collaboration of unlike minds—including scientists, politicians, and businesspeople—that led to a solution that at first seemed unreachable, Abigail noted. In 2023, a United Nations report announced that the ozone layer was healing and that it was on track to recover within four decades.[15]

As many experts on creativity have recognized, *not* knowing much about a subject can be a great instigator of novel ideas, particularly when it is combined with the power of expertise. Abigail herself is an example of this. She came to Google with a Harvard degree in anthropology and professional experience in the advertising world. She didn't know a whole lot about technology, and that was the point.

When Abigail arrived at Google, she came to see that the company was receiving loads of data about what people were doing online, but not as much knowledge about *why*. Using her anthropology and advertising background has helped the company close that gap between what and why.

Another thing about Abigail, which she readily admits, is that she's something of a ham: She enjoyed acting in plays in her younger days. Google executives quickly realized that they could harness her stage presence to Google's advantage by encouraging her to pursue opportunities to express her ideas to clients and other groups; through speeches, her ideas about creativity and the digital landscape could have more impact.

As Abigail put it, "I couldn't compartmentalize myself. I would have failed." First she combined unlike notions in her own thinking, and then she extended that expansiveness to others on her teams. That meant getting to know the many sides of her team members—their hobbies, their interests, their backgrounds, their previous work experience—not just for the sake of making chitchat, but because there is genuine value to be derived from this knowledge.

People then have a sense of their own value: "What I have to offer matters. Not because I have this one lane of thinking.

But because I have this extended sense of myself, whether it's because I studied ballet, or learned Greek, or I'm a great mother, or ran a marathon. My whole self is being embraced. Which makes them feel more heard, but you actually become more innovative as a result. And it's innovation that only your team can exhibit, because only your team has this combination of people with these different sides."

A big part of Abigail's job is to help advertisers run the most effective advertising and branded content possible. Analysts on her team have developed best practices for various types of advertising channels, but she sometimes has trouble convincing clients to go with a different approach. Using the usual routes, such as an oral or slide presentation, doesn't always cut it.

As it happens, one of her analysts is a prolific traveler who creates YouTube videos featuring highlights of his journeys, such as erupting volcanoes in Iceland. When one particular client was reluctant to give the go-ahead on a new idea, the analyst decided to produce a rudimentary YouTube video as a "proof of concept" to show how the proposed new advertising would look. The client saw the video and was sold. "When they see it come to life, it's harder for them to say no," Abigail said.

This approach was so successful that the team decided to turn it into a whole new sales offering. The analyst reached out to a former journalist on Abigail's strategy team to write marketing materials for the new services so that it could be effectively communicated to clients.

When you embrace your own expansiveness, "and then when you do it with others on the team, it becomes much more of an opportunity to really enhance the innovation," Abigail said.

GE activated the power of its incredibly diverse businesses when it came up with new products during the "Imagination at Work" era. The company's health-care division knew it had a problem with its anesthesia machines, which were so complicated and distracting with various dials and beeping noises that it was hard for anesthesiologists to concentrate on their jobs.

As former GE Chief Marketing Officer Beth Comstock recalled in her book *Imagine It Forward*, "So people at GE asked: 'Who else finds themselves in such life and death situations, navigating all kinds of inputs and monitoring equipment?' And they had a startlingly useful realization: An airplane's cockpit is remarkably similar to an operating room. So they invited pilots to observe surgeries and help GE identify the problems. That turned out to be fairly easy, as their industry had faced an almost identical problem years before." The strategy worked, and with the pilots' help, GE's engineers designed a new and improved machine.

You can't see a jar's label from inside the jar, Comstock noted. Therefore, "We had to get 'outside the jar.'"[16]

TRY A DIET WORKOUT

Our WorkOuts at BBDO are one way to harness the power of diverse backgrounds and unlike notions. While highly effective, they can involve a serious investment of time and money, and they may not always be feasible. But you could put a kind of diet WorkOut in motion right now, simply by gathering together a group of people (up to a dozen—any more than that can be unwieldy) from different levels and different departments within your organization.

Bring them to a separate space, remove any big tables, and set their wheels turning on a creative challenge of your choosing. Don't just open the floor to ideas in general—that's a sure way to generate lots of complaints. Make sure you put serious thought into giving them a highly specific and clearly defined challenge to address—one that, if solved, could truly bring your business to a new level. And tell them what that challenge is in advance. (I'll discuss some of this—such as the reasoning behind removing the tables, and how to design a specific challenge—in more detail in future chapters.)

When the meeting begins, the leader of the group can start things off by offering several mediocre or bad ideas. As I have noted, the secret to finding creative new ideas is to generate lots of bad ideas first. If the group leader throws out some stupid ideas as an opener, then others in the group will feel emboldened to share their own thoughts, and then after a time the bad ideas will organically dissolve to reveal good ones.

Inevitably, you will encounter some form of negativity and skepticism during your search for creative new ideas. All organizations employ curmudgeons, and most of us harbor a curmudgeonly impulse that causes us to say, "That will never work," or, "We've always done it this way."

If someone asserts that a particular idea could not possibly work, reframe it by asking what's good about the idea, and what it would take to make it work. This is known as the "yes, and" approach. No idea is ever perfect. If you focus solely on the imperfections, you may well end up dismissing your best ideas because you're looking at them through the wrong lens.

You need to understand that the cognitive urge to deselect, as a way of narrowing down a profusion of choices, is strong. The best way to do your diet WorkOut would be to look at ten ideas with the goal of coming up with the three strongest ones. But the leader should do it with "yes, and" input from the group, and by then selecting the three that have the most potential to become great. This is a much more positive and useful method than deselecting the seven that supposedly could never work.

Not only does this approach have the potential to uncover new creative opportunities, but it also signals that you believe that people throughout the organization—in all departments and at all levels—are capable of generating ideas. Because they truly are.

6

STEP ONE
OF THE SHIFT

The Right Question

Before they start work, ad agency creative teams receive what's called a brief, which defines the audience the client is trying to reach, the change in behavior they're trying to create, and the message and supporting evidence the agency should use to do it.

You'd think copywriters would like the brief to be as empty a page of paper as possible. The proverbial blank sheet of paper. Creativity unleashed!

Getting down to work, however, one quickly realizes that constraints—like concrete objectives and fixed deadlines—make the Creative Shift easier to pull off. In fact, there's an old advertising mantra that goes, "God give me the freedom of a tight brief." Meaning, please give me some limits!

The problem to be solved is the chief constraint. Therefore, defining the problem is the most important first step toward the Creative Shift. It's also the step most often skipped or done poorly. Flabby, generic statements of problems are somehow both overwhelming and uninspiring. While something like "saving the planet" in the abstract is important, it's useless as a creative prompt.

It's critical to pare down and refine a given problem to a compelling conundrum that will drive the Creative Shift—a question so piercing that it elicits answering sparks from anyone who hears it. A well-defined problem is ambitious, even daunting, yet stripped to something so vital and inspiring that you can't help toying with it in your mind like an addictive puzzle.

In 1943, the inventor Edwin Land was on vacation in Santa Fe, New Mexico, when he took a picture of his daughter Jennifer, who was three years old at the time.[1] When he told her she was going to have to wait to see the photo, she impatiently said, "Why can't I see it right now?"

At the time, people had to bring the film from their cameras to a photo lab where it could be professionally developed, with technicians bathing the film in trays of chemicals inside a darkroom. Getting the photos back could take a few days. But Jennifer didn't know that, and so she felt free to ask a question that most adults at the time would have considered naïve, though of course cutely excusable in such a young child.

Not Edwin Land. Jennifer's question served as a bolt of inspiration to him. Why indeed, he thought. "Within an hour, the camera, the film, and the physical chemistry became so clear" to him, Land recalled, that he contacted his patent attorney and began working on the invention that became known as the Polaroid Land camera.

In this day and age, we take for granted that we can immediately see the photos we take digitally on our phones. But at the time, it was revolutionary for people to be able to snap a photo and soon see it emerge from the camera, with the chemical processes having begun to occur inside the machine.

"Why can't we see photos now?" is an example of a truly well-defined problem. Some might find it remarkable that it came from a three-year-old. But as I pointed out in the previous chapter, children, and toddlers especially, are in many ways more imaginative than adults, because their brains have not yet become filled with all the assumptions and prohibitions of adulthood.

As Steve Jobs is frequently credited with saying, "If you define the problem correctly, you almost have the solution."

THE FREEDOM OF TIGHT CONSTRAINTS

At BBDO we always begin the creative process by paring the problem down to its essence. Sakichi Toyoda, the legendary

Japanese inventor whose son founded Toyota, asked "why" five times when facing a tough problem.[2] Each *why* got him closer to the underlying cause. This discipline clears away ugly guidelines and gets you to a useful set of constraints.

Elon Musk pared rocket development down to its essential elements through a series of questions. He insisted that his engineers question every specification. As Walter Isaacson writes in his biography of Musk, "Whenever one of his engineers cited 'a requirement' as a reason for doing something, Musk would grill them: Who made that requirement? And answering 'The military' or 'The legal department' was not good enough. Musk would insist that they know the name of the actual person who made the requirement." Every specification should be considered a mere recommendation. For Musk, according to Isaacson, "the only immutable" requirements were the ones "decreed by the laws of physics."[3]

A few years ago, Ford tasked BBDO with launching the Mustang Mach-E, an all-electric vehicle that did not yet exist. Quite an advertising challenge. Complicating the job further, we weren't supposed to sell the Mach-E to current Mustang owners. This meant it required thinking way outside the norm.

Ford's market research indicated that current Mustang owners weren't interested in electric cars. Instead, the company hoped to use the new car to win over electric-curious customers who wouldn't ordinarily consider a Mustang. The question we needed to answer was how to get people who didn't buy Mustangs to buy a Mustang that hasn't even been made yet? Or, put another way, how do you convince people to roll the dice on a Ford instead of a Tesla?

Advertising agencies often become weighed down with "ugly guidelines." An ugly guideline here might have been, "The car needs to be shot from a low, three-quarter angle." Or "the ad has to feature the electric vehicle's lack of a front grille." Ugly guidelines don't unlock problems. They tie your hands, forcing you to add when you need to subtract.

Similarly, an objective like "increase penetration of the Ford brand using its new electric Mustang" does nothing useful. Framing a problem purely in terms of its urgency and importance is ineffective and lazy. Defining an effective prompt takes work, but, as you'll see, solving an interesting problem tends to achieve all the objectives along the way.

For the Mustang Mach-E, the creative team generated and then ruthlessly culled different formulations in search of a prompt that got to the heart of the matter. Eventually, they distilled the challenge as follows: *Get people who think of Ford as an old-fashioned brand to buy a cutting-edge product that doesn't yet exist with almost no media money.*

Once we landed on this problem, the juices started flowing. Blunt, clear, and bracing, it suggested the need for a campaign that felt new, fresh, and vital. No falling back on nostalgia. No home movie footage of Mom driving her 1968 Mustang California Special to the grocery store.

How do you sell a product that doesn't exist? Simulate it. At BBDO, we always stay on top of the latest media technologies. Products like Magic Leap and Oculus, with their headsets and special cameras, had brought lifelike virtual reality closer, but the market penetration wasn't there yet. (Another constraint.) We didn't stop there, however. In lieu of truly immersive VR, we developed a compelling mobile experience on Instagram that allowed prospective customers to explore a virtual Mach-E while listening to designers and engineers describing the vehicle's merits. Though the car hadn't been built, this virtual walkthrough convinced 20,000 people to put down $500 deposits—a $10 million kick start for what became *Car and Driver's* first EV of the Year, for 2021, beating out Tesla.

Creativity happens in leaps, not steps. Ideas crystallize in an instant. Most leaders don't realize, however, the need for extensive preparation beforehand. Great ideas don't have to be scarce. It's well-framed problems that are more likely to be scarce. If you want better ideas, ruthlessly pare your problem down to the sharpest possible prompt. Then, watch the Creative Shift happen as light bulbs appear out of nowhere. With the right prompt, it's hard *not* to have ideas.

FOR BIG IDEAS, START SMALL

In 2004, the British grocery store chain Sainsbury's sought help for a serious problem: The company had slipped to third place in the United Kingdom, a symptom of plummeting customer satisfaction. The solution? Increase annual sales by £2.5 billion over three years. Somehow.

Boring! Show me a company that *doesn't* want to increase sales. A tepid brief like this wouldn't get us anywhere big, and to drive billions in additional sales, we'd need a whopper of an idea. You won't hit that ninth zero with incremental tinkering.

To get a big idea, start small. For Sainsbury's, we went granular: the shopping cart. Crunching the numbers, we found that an average gain of £1.14 per shopper per week would meet Sainsbury's growth target. In other words, we needed one additional item for every customer on every trip to the grocery store. Reframing the problem this way made things more interesting. Instead of struggling to convince patrons of other supermarket chains to switch, we just needed to convince every Sainsbury's shopper to put one more thing in their shopping cart. Simple, though fiendishly difficult.

Time for some careful observation. Team members shadowed Sainsbury's shoppers: "I remember one woman very clearly," recalled Craig Mawdsley, BBDO's joint head of planning at the time. "We were walking around the store. I was asking her questions about what she bought, how often she came, whether she shopped with a list, and whom she was buying for. I came to realize that she was shopping on automatic pilot, what we later dubbed 'sleep-shopping.'"

Sleep-shopping? Even more interesting. How would we get people to add an item to their cart when they were half-asleep in the aisles? Clearly, we'd need to wake shoppers up!

There's a classic experiment in the social sciences.[4] Participants watch a video to count the number of times a ball is passed back and forth by a group of people. Halfway through the video, a person in a gorilla suit walks right into the middle of the scene, bangs on his chest, and exits.

After the video ends, participants are asked whether they noticed the gorilla in the room. *What gorilla?* Most observers have been so focused on counting ball passes that they've missed the gorilla entirely.

During our brainstorming process, this odd little finding snapped together with the sleep-shopping insight. We decided to call attention to the phenomenon of sleep-shopping by performing our own variation on the gorilla experiment. In BBDO's award-winning campaign, a gorilla joins the throngs of weeknight shoppers at a Sainsbury's supermarket. As predicted by research, the shoppers remain blissfully unaware.

"There's a million meals to choose from," celebrity chef Jamie Oliver tells viewers during the spot. "Why eat the same ones again and again?" The core idea of the "Try Something New" campaign was to snap shoppers out of their usual routine by offering simple recipes that required one or two unfamiliar ingredients. Grating nutmeg onto spaghetti Bolognese, for example, or adding watercress to a sausage sandwich. Customers welcomed the opportunity to add another £1.14 or so to their grocery bill this way because it led to surprising new culinary experiences. The ads—along with recipe cards distributed across all stores—were received not as a sales pitch but as a service.

The new recipes didn't simply boost sales for the listed ingredients. Sainsbury's saw a general lift in sales across each store. The campaign became so successful that the company began winning customers from other chains, restoring it to second place in the nation. (As I said earlier, solving interesting problems has a way of hitting all the objectives along the way.) The campaign was an extraordinarily effective example of mass behavior change, and it was all possible because we had invested so much energy in asking a better question.

HOW TO CREATE PROVOCATIVE PROMPTS

The principles behind our WorkOuts can be used to attack nearly any creative problem with a team. To run an effective session, however, you will need to create a set of prompts based on the defined problem.

Recently, we were asked to pitch Desperados, a lager with the distilled spirit "aguardiente" that is owned by Heineken and sold in dozens of countries globally. Heineken's core objective was to grow the brand—isn't it always?—but that requirement wouldn't get us anywhere useful. Only specific, provocative prompts stimulate the kinds of actionable ideas that achieve the big predictable ones like brand growth.

To win the business, we began by defining audience segments and estimating the size of each one. For Desperados, the chief target was "adults between legal drinking age and twenty-five." But useful segments are about more than just demographics. For example, we learned that one in five customers drink Desperados at home to "pre-game" before heading out for the evening. "Pre-gamers" is a much more useful segment to consider when framing your question. If the way you think about your audience isn't leading anywhere interesting, go beyond simple markers like age, gender, or profession and dig into context, location, and other factors.

To drill deeper, we identify three "truths" to triangulate our position: the truth of the audience (market), the truth of the brand (product), and the truth of the moment (zeitgeist). In the case of Desperados, the truth of the audience was that Desperados drinkers aren't as wild and uninhibited as you might expect of people who consume beer with tequila in it. These drinkers are adventurous in theory but cautious and conventional in practice.

The truth of the brand was that Desperados beer contains a small amount of "aguardiente"—a distilled alcoholic spirit that gives it a little more kick than the average lager. The truth of the moment for these drinkers, as we found out in focus group research, was that they struggled to navigate a culture that no longer told them who to be or how to act. All the old rules felt obsolete. This generation saw itself as culturally adrift.

With our three truths settled, we started looking for a connection or tension between them to guide our efforts. Over the course of this discussion, we landed on the idea of Desperados as "the party beer whose special ingredient, aguardiente, gives a cautious generation the momentum to embrace the unexpected and claim the youth you only get to live once." This strategic push to "keep the young, young" would serve as the overriding theme of the brief we brought to a three-day WorkOut.

Desperados drinkers are youthful, but they don't behave that way. They're guarded. Uncertain. By lowering their inhibitions, Desperados could help them relax and enjoy themselves.

Having defined our strategic push, we used everything we'd learned about the audience, the brand, and the culture to define specific prompts. For example, since most people consumed Desperados at home, increasing bar consumption was the lowest-hanging fruit. This led us to a prompt to identify new drinking rituals. In a bar, the social aspects of drinking are on display.

One way to stand out when everyone is holding a bottle is through a ritual attached to that brand. The wedge of lime helped make Corona one of the most valuable beer brands in the world. For Desperados, one idea we eventually generated was to tap the bottom of a friend's bottle with the bottom of yours, causing their beer to foam up and forcing them to drink quickly to keep it from spilling on the floor. That would get the party started.

Another prompt: The Nigerian diaspora celebrates Detty December, a Christmas-related festival. "How might Desperados own Detty December wherever Nigerians live?" This prompt was useful because Detty December is a unique, interesting, and popular cultural phenomenon. Also, it would torture-test the idea of tying Desperados to specific cultural celebrations. If a targeted campaign worked for Detty December, it might work for other seasonal celebrations as well.

Another prompt: What do you do to stand out in a market like France where, by law, in advertising alcoholic drinks, you can only talk about the product's origin and/

or manufacturing process? How do you "keep the young, young" with such a tight constraint? Previously, for another alcoholic beverage expanding into France, I'd suggested hiring naked tasters to work in the distillery so that we could feature them on billboards. (The brand didn't end up doing it, which is probably for the best.) Region-specific restrictions like this are another good source of useful creative prompts.

Many prompts arise directly from the specific strategic challenge you've identified. However, there is always an overlap between related problems, so you can establish a template if you're usually solving similar creative problems. A Work-Out on one car brand will contain some of the same prompts as one performed on another.

For a WorkOut, it's helpful to assemble a mix of old and new, familiar prompts and fresh ones. A three-day WorkOut will contain roughly six sprints, timed sessions in which the teams must respond to a prompt. Prepare at least that many prompts before assembling your teams.

When brainstorming fails, it's usually because the prompts weren't prepared before the session started. Too often, leaders assemble a group on the fly and then wonder why nothing happens. The creative process should be free, loose, informal, and fun. But this happens only through rigorous and meticulous preparation beforehand.

Sometimes, the prompts just don't come. Your problem remains frustratingly opaque despite everyone's best efforts, and energy starts to run low. If you're not careful, the team can get, to put it bluntly, disgruntled.

When it comes to creativity, the danger is rarely failure. There's almost always *something* you can do, something you can run with. The real risk is going with an inferior solution because you've run out of time, or energy, or both. For world-class results, settling must be avoided at all costs. But how do you avoid "okay" when frustration mounts? How do you reinvigorate a brainstorm that only drizzles?

"Never chase after opponents," the legendary Japanese martial artist Morihei Ueshiba warned.[5] Ueshiba, the creator of the Japanese martial art aikido, was referring to the challenge of hand-to-hand combat against a nimble foe, but we've all experienced a problem that keeps dancing out of our grasp. Some are tough nuts to crack, but others are just *slippery*. You think you've made progress by solving one part, only to realize you've introduced a new wrinkle in another. Rinse and repeat, round and round. This is what happens when you haven't yet reduced the problem to its distinct essence. You will chase that stubborn problem around the ring to the point of utter exhaustion without ever laying a hand on it. Then, you'll tap out with a good-enough solution—to everyone's eventual regret.

How do you catch a slippery opponent? "Redirect each attack," Ueshiba advised, "and get firmly behind it." In other words, stop chasing and surrender. Instead of putting more energy into an approach that isn't working, take a step back and use the slipperiness of the problem against itself. Reframe your obstacles as opportunities: "What isn't working here, and why is that actually a good thing?" For example, Avis made a strength of Hertz's dominance of the rental car category with the simple slogan "We try harder." This is creative aikido in action.

TURNING WEAKNESS INTO STRENGTH

Bayer makes aspirin, also known as acetylsalicylic acid. An aspirin precursor found in willow tree bark has been used for its health benefits for 2,400 years, and Bayer Aspirin itself was first synthesized in 1897.

Bayer Aspirin's benefits aren't specific to any one malady: It reduces pain. It reduces inflammation. It thins the blood. It can help treat anything from Kawasaki disease to pericarditis to rheumatic fever, all while helping ward off heart attacks, stroke, and blood clots. It may not seem to be the best, most modern option for every medical problem, but the fact that it does so many things so well makes it a legitimate wonder.

(Ironically, aspirin's creator synthesized what he thought would be a "hero" drug eleven days later: a less-addictive form of morphine. While he was right on aspirin, he was dead wrong on heroin.)

Bayer Aspirin's versatility makes it a remarkable boon for humanity, but, if you'll pardon the irony, it can be a pain in the neck for BBDO and Bayer's marketing teams. Every alternative medicine in every medical niche where it competes has been "tailor-made" for that condition. If you need a blood thinner, your doctor may give you Coumadin. If you need an anti-inflammatory, you reach for Aleve. Aspirin's opposition is everywhere, and each opponent boasts impeccable positioning. So while Bayer Aspirin is the jack of all medical trades, it can be seen as the master of none.

For a new campaign in Mexico, BBDO chased this problem around the ring until everyone at the table needed a, well, what do you take for a headache? Normally, we ask, "What is this product best at?" and "How do we bring that to life in an ad?" Rather than capitulate, we tried creative aikido by flipping the usual formulation: "What is this product's biggest weakness?" and "How could we use that weakness to persuade people to buy it?"

Bayer Aspirin's problem could be that it's seen as a good remedy for many ailments, rather than the "go to" for anything in particular. But it could be reframed as being *great* at being a good option, a unique strength, particularly in a market like Mexico where access to expensive, cutting-edge medical care is rarely fast, easy, or affordable. This insight led us to an idea: "Bayer Aspirin: The World's Smallest First-Aid Kit."

Like gauze or cotton, it can be counted on in many situations that occur without warning and leave little time to call a doctor, get a prescription written, and find a pharmacy to fill it—sometimes in the middle of the night. If you need immediate help for anything from a headache to a heart attack, you can count on Bayer Aspirin. The campaign successfully highlighted the elegance of the product's broad utility. If that tiny white pill can address such a wide array of problems, it only makes sense to keep a bottle in your medicine cabinet. Or even your pocket, just in case.

In many ways, Guinness faced the opposite problem as Bayer Aspirin: Arguably, there is no beer as distinctive as the famous Irish stout. Yet creative aikido proved just as useful for Guinness as it did for Bayer.

"Guinness is an extraordinary brand," wrote Colin Storm, Guinness's managing director in Great Britain. "It is hard to think of a beer which over two centuries has been held in such affection and has, to many around the world, come to symbolize a way of life."[6]

Ironically, it was Storm who, days later, asked our British agency to help change that way of life. It would have been perfectly reasonable to question Storm's sanity. Guinness had everything a beer brand might want: a delicious, malty flavor, as anyone who has enjoyed one can confirm; an unmistakable appearance, with its thick, creamy head; a rich advertising heritage with countless memorable and beloved campaigns; and admiration, even reverence, from both casual drinkers and beer aficionados around the world as an iconic Irish beverage.

Despite all that admiration, however—or, more accurately, because of it—Guinness wasn't enjoyed frequently enough. People knew what Guinness was and what it was for: a quiet conversation in a cozy pub. A rich accompaniment to a plate of fish and chips. The occasional restorative pint after a game of soccer. The rest of the time—most of the time—young men turned to beer that would stimulate a buzzy, upbeat mood. "Session drinking" was where the volume was in the industry, and that category was dominated by lager brands that looked the same, tasted the same, and largely advertised in the exact same way.

To free Guinness from its cozy image, we had to change its mellow mood to one that was a bit more *charged*. In theory, there was no reason this couldn't work. Empirically, we knew people drank Guinness at rugby matches and on St. Patrick's Day. The mellow association was just a matter of perception. What would it take to change that perception of Guinness across the board?

When asked what they remembered about Guinness advertising, everyone, and I mean everyone, responded with the same famous tagline: Guinness is good for you. This was an inextricable part of the brand lore. In the past, Great Britain's National Health Service had given hospital patients Guinness daily because of its high iron count. Attitudes toward alcohol had changed in the intervening years, however, and there was simply no way we could bring that slogan back.

Wait a second—that was a weakness, wasn't it?

How might we leverage the power of "Guinness is good for you" without using the line itself?

Another weakness: It takes 119 seconds to pour a perfect pint of Guinness. Three steps that take almost two full minutes. As delicious as a properly poured pint can be, this can be difficult to tolerate. The wait doesn't matter when you're winding down for a contemplative chat in a charming little bar, but it can be a drag when getting the party started with friends on a raucous Thursday night.

"How might we *use* the wait to position Guinness as the perfect 'charge-up' pint?"

As often happens with creative aikido, the weaknesses we'd identified complemented each other beautifully.

Waiting isn't always a weakness. Sometimes, waiting builds anticipation, winding you up instead of winding things down. Suspense can sharpen even the most positive experience, building a nervous energy that only climaxes with the anticipated event. Whether you're a kid waiting for Christmas Day or a grown-up waiting for the kick-off, looking forward to something eagerly adds intensity to the reward that is lost with instant gratification.

How do you flip that switch, however? How do you turn a delay into anticipation?

That's where our thinking dovetailed with our second problem: "Guinness is good for you." Maybe not, but it is *good*. And you know what they say . . .

"Good Things Come to Those Who Wait" leveraged the extraordinary brand equity of "Guinness is good for you" without crossing any regulatory lines while making a virtue out of what had been seen as both a practical and an emotional barrier.

In one representative ad from that campaign, Marco, the village hero, swims across the bay in a race against the pouring of a pint of Guinness. The viewer is drawn into the anticipation as his fellow villagers cheer Marco on. Through sleight of hand, Marco's bar-owning brother ensures Marco's victory—and the evening of Guinness-fueled revelry that follows.

The "Good Things Come to Those Who Wait" campaign was extraordinarily successful, increasing brand penetration, frequency of usage, and market share.

PLEASE DON'T USE OUR PRODUCT

We also encouraged customers to wait in a set of ads we did for AT&T. Except in this case we actively, and somewhat paradoxically, strongly urged people *not to use* their phones. And to point out that most of what people send over their phones isn't even all that important.

The purpose of this counterintuitive messaging? To prevent texting and posting while driving. We saw that distracted driving caused more accidents than drunk driving, and yet 70 percent of people reported that they used their phones behind the wheel. And we understood that many drivers think that accidents due to distracted driving happen to *other* people, not them. How to change their behavior? We sought to do that by airing several commercials that showed people going about their daily routines and then finding their lives permanently altered because of a single post or text.

We did research in which we asked people to look up their most recent texts and posts, and got them to realize that almost all of them truly *could* wait. In another commercial, we got actual drivers to sheepishly and even laughingly confess that they often texted or used social media while driving. "If someone texts you, you can't just let it sit there without knowing what someone said," says one woman. "What if something exciting's happening?" says another woman. Says one man, "Every time I do it I think, why am I doing this? And then I just keep doing it."

Then these people meet a partially paralyzed woman who tells them she was riding home from her college graduation ceremony when an 18-wheeler crashed into her car trying to avoid a distracted driver who was running a red light. Both her parents were killed and she spent two months in the hospital, followed by two months of rehab learning to walk and speak again. The reactions of the drivers to her story are powerful and palpable.

As a result of the campaign, millions of people signed an "It Can Wait" pledge, promising not to text while driving.

It was quite a dramatic shift to go out and tell people, "Please don't use your phone." But it was actually incredibly powerful in terms of the way people felt about the AT&T brand. It made clear that the culture of AT&T is one of supreme responsibility for people and their well-being.

The next time you find yourself circling a problem rather than seizing it, cut the frontal assault short and look for ways to turn a negative force into a positive one: creative aikido.

For people to be at their most creative, you need to remove everything that gets in the way—distractions, stressors, any sense of judgment or criticism—and add everything that stimulates fresh thinking. Here, we've seen how asking the right questions is key to making the Creative Shift by spurring interesting and valuable lines of thought in any group of people. Indeed, how you start affects the quality of how you end the creative process. In the next chapter, I'll show you how to create an environment where ideas will be sparked and nurtured over time.

7

PRIMING THE BRAIN FOR BREAKTHROUGHS

When you've done something before, your brain has a road map of what to do, but the Creative Shift requires the freedom to wander. Ideas need exposure to new raw materials. Data are clearly an important place to start, but you need more than that. Creative leaps in the brain are often fueled by direct observation. The more you can graze, the more you can grow.

Creative breakthroughs also happen more readily when you make it a point to consciously stop thinking about a puzzling problem for a while. I encourage our people to take walks, meditate, listen to music or a podcast, or just sit and stare off into space for a few minutes, because I know that these mental rests allow the wheels to turn in the back of their heads without their even being conscious of it happening.

More than any other distinguishing trait, prolific creative people look, listen, and ponder longer. They're patient and curious, often directing their attention at peripheral aspects of a problem that others dismiss as irrelevant. Rather than fearing tangents, creators delight in them.

If you keep your eyes and ears and your mind open, you will find yourself having more ideas. It's as simple as that.

And never underestimate the value of observations that accrue over time. Sometimes your discoveries will yield a half-formed idea that ends up incubating in your brain for a long while before it receives just the right internal or external push. I call this "soaking."

One of the executive creative directors I worked with has an extreme approach toward this aspect of problem-solving. Whenever he happens to see something that sparks his interest—say, a clever video or a new technology—he makes a note of it and thinks, "There must be a way for me to use this." In this way, he's constantly looking for solutions to questions that haven't been asked yet. And when the question finally *does* get asked, maybe quite a while later, he's ready to pounce.

He saw the huge potential of virtual reality long before it became popular. He kept wondering how he could use the concept when VR's market penetration was still too small to be useful. As we saw in the preceding chapter, when Mustang was trying to get people to buy the Mach-E before it existed, he found a way to simulate a VR experience of the Mach-E on Instagram. This led 20,000 people to put down a deposit on the still-to-be-launched car.

In his book *Where Good Ideas Come From*, the innovation expert and best-selling author Steven Johnson talks about the importance of quietly nurturing the "slow hunch" over time.

"The snap judgments of intuition—as powerful as they can be—are rarities in the history of world-changing ideas," Johnson writes. "Most hunches that turn into important innovations unfold over much longer time frames. They start with a vague, hard-to-describe sense that there's an interesting solution to a problem that hasn't been proposed, and they linger in the shadows of the mind, sometimes for decades, assembling new connections and gaining strength."[1] These slow hunches need the fullness of time to evolve to their full potential, and it is all too easy for them to become crushed by the demands of daily life, he warns.

Facebook, one of the biggest new ideas of the past two decades, was essentially a long, slow hunch. As Mark Zuckerberg, its founder, said in his 2017 commencement address at Harvard University, "Ideas don't come out fully formed. They only become clear as you work on them. You just have to get started. If I had to understand everything about connecting people before I began, I never would have started Facebook."[2]

"The idea of a single eureka moment is a dangerous lie," he added. "It makes us feel inadequate since we haven't had ours. It prevents people with seeds of good ideas from getting started."

Steven Johnson notes that some creative geniuses like to recall their breakthrough moments as sudden epiphanies, the equivalent of the apple falling on Newton's head.[3] Despite the "narrative thrill" of their recollections, historical detective work often shows that "the slow hunch is the rule, not the exception," he writes.

An intellectual historian who closely examined Charles Darwin's notebooks, for example, found that the theory of natural selection had been building slowly (evolving, even) in Darwin's mind for a year before he put all the pieces together based on various separate observations he had made. This was contrary to the eureka moment that Darwin described in his own autobiography.

GO FORTH AND EXPLORE

To stimulate ideas, one of the most powerful actions leaders can take is to invite people to be modern-day Darwins and put themselves out in the world. For Don Draper in *Mad Men*, this could mean heading to a cinema during the workday. We encourage such forays at BBDO. What does seeing a movie have to do with selling soda? Plenty. Movies both reflect and create culture, and only culture can explain why people prefer a certain soda when they can't even spot it in a taste test. (For proof, google "New Coke.")

To make the Creative Shift, go foraging. Observe. Take notes.

Just look at my father, who was a plant manager in South Africa for Nestlé, which made (and still makes) Milo chocolate malt powder. Now, according to the directions, you're supposed to add the powder to hot or cold milk. But back in the 1970s my dad observed that quite a few people, including his own children, had a habit of scooping the powder directly out of the can and eating it dry. That's how tasty it was.

That led him to an idea that apparently hadn't occurred either to the marketers of Milo or to the innovation people working on Nestlé chocolate. Why not turn the powder into a chocolate bar? His factory in South Africa had an experimental kitchen lab and he set to work making some prototypes, with a mold that already existed for other Nestlé chocolate bars (thereby keeping costs down). From there he tested the prototypes on his Milo-loving kids. And then he went to the head office in Johannesburg with the kid-tested winner and said, "Here, try this" (yet another great example of starting at the end rather than the beginning).

I was delighted—and felt a renewed pride in my father fifty years later—to see a Milo bar in a basket in a conference room in one of our offices in Australia. I hadn't seen one in quite some time and wasn't sure they were still being made.

Maybe I was channeling a bit of my father when we were charged with trying to help increase sales of Campbell's Soup. The perennial problem for Campbell's has not been that people don't buy cans of soup. They do. Usually quite a few. The problem is that they then don't *open* the cans. They sit in the larder for months. Sometimes years. If you survey customers about this, their answers are useless: "The soup is there in case I need it. Or if I get sick." Or "It's a backup in case the fridge breaks." Short of infecting them with a virus or sabotaging their major appliances, the research tells us little except that people actually like the soup. So why don't they consume it?

Observe someone's kitchen, and the answer becomes clear. What's the first thing you do upon entering your own kitchen? You open the fridge. What's more, you probably open the fridge every time you walk through the kitchen. Canned soup sits in the cabinet. In there, it might as well be in an offsite warehouse. People forget about it.

That's why yogurt became so successful in America. It's versatile—breakfast, snack, dessert—and it *goes in the fridge*, where it gets seen constantly. When preparing a meal, most people don't consult a recipe. They open the fridge, look to see what's there, and figure out what they can rustle up. Shelf-stable soups are an advantage for Campbell's in the store but a barrier to usage in the home.

This observation led us to a question: If canned soup doesn't need to be in the fridge, how do you get it there anyway? Our idea: a plastic cap that you could put on top of an opened can and store in the fridge. (They never ended up making a plastic cap, but that's what happens to even the best ideas sometimes.)

Look everywhere. Watch customers interacting with your brand and your competitors' brands. Watch them in different contexts altogether and seek parallels. And be aware that your background, and your cultural references, may be quite different from those of the customers or clients you are trying to reach.

ACT LIKE AN ANTHROPOLOGIST

To get outside the walls of your own expertise and assumptions, it can be very helpful to behave like a consumer anthropologist, observing people in their natural habitats. This means noticing how they behave online, in their homes, and in stores.

"My goal is to make consumers feel more familiar to brand teams so these teams can figure out how to surprise and delight them," said Gina Fong, a consumer anthropologist and assistant marketing professor at the Kellogg School of Management in Evanston, Illinois.[4] Her field exists to address "the *why* behind people's choices," she told *Kellogg Insight*, a school publication.

"When you look at consumer behavior, it's like there's a firewall between people's behavior and the motivation behind it," she said, "and you've got to break through that firewall."

For example, she helped a maker of garbage bags understand why a small segment of buyers was willing to pay two to three times what the average consumers would pay for a particular type of bag. She discovered that these people lived in either walk-up apartment buildings or large apartment complexes, and that these bags were the least likely to tear or leak when they were carried across a hallway or down flights of stairs. She came to understand the repercussions experienced by people who turn back from the Dumpster or the trash room to see a long line of coffee grounds or cat litter form a trail back to their door.

"If their trash bag broke at any point in the process, they would be at least 20 minutes late to work," said Fong. "For them, the trash bag was an investment in their ability to start their day on the right foot."

Based on observations like these, brands are able to come up with new products, services, and campaigns that have consumers saying, "You get me," Fong said.

That's how a colleague of hers felt when he visited a store that divided its avocados into categories with three signs: "ripe today," "ripe in a couple of days," and "ripe in four to five days." The man had given up on avocados because he could never get the timing right between too firm and too mushy. The store had entered into his experience and understood his dilemma, which is surely true for many others, and he started buying avocados again.

An article in *The Economist* noted that the great Argentine soccer player Lionel Messi surveys the field fifty times a minute.[5] During an entire World Cup, he ran less than all but one player—that is, he didn't actually run up and down the field that much; in terms of running distance, he was almost at the bottom, with only one player beating him for the least amount of running. Instead of running farther or faster, Messi carefully observed the field. He moved only when he needed to, and when he did move, he moved to the exact spot that he needed to be in to contribute to the game in the ways that have made him such a legendary soccer player. Because he runs less, he has more energy when he needs it and is one pace faster than his opponents.

Too often, companies dive into "innovation" without taking enough time to fully understand the problem they are trying to solve. For better ideas, spend less time running and more time watching. Leave the fortress of your own mind and see the creative possibilities expand.

I love to travel to other countries for this very reason. When I go to Japan, for example, I'm constantly amazed by the quality of the packaging. The way even a piece of chocolate is wrapped is breathtaking. I can't just rip it open and eat it; I need to examine and admire it first.

And I'm not a huge beer drinker, but Japan has installed automated beer-pouring machines in places like airport lounges that tilt the glass to the perfect angle and fill it to the perfect spot, exactly the way an experienced bartender would pour it. When I'm in Japan I drink beer just so I can marvel at these precision-engineered machines.

I've also noticed that certain cities are much more creative at billboards and street advertising than others. Shanghai, for one, is spectacular at creating 3D electronic billboards. Their newer building infrastructure makes the billboards easier to install than in the past, and the last time I was there I was awestruck by how artistic and immersive these displays were.

And in Paris recently, I marveled that Louis Vuitton had found a way to conceal renovation work on its first hotel, on the Champs-Élysées, with a simulation of a giant aluminum Louis Vuitton trunk. The magnificent spectacle (which was later replicated at a construction site in New York) made its way onto social media posts around the world. (The company was probably not so thrilled that the image attracted the attention of the activists who placed a giant banner across the trunk with the words "TAX THE RICH," to draw attention to wealth disparities, but their customers and potential customers around the world probably didn't mind.)

I travel to BBDO offices around the world not only to see what our people are doing, but also to see what our competitors are doing. And wherever I am, I look at things that are being done brilliantly in *any* category and try to imagine ways to translate them into what our company or clients do. Because ultimately, that's what we're going to need to beat.

Amazon, for one, raised the bar much higher when it set up a system that enabled an array of products—household goods, clothing, and personal care products, to name just a few—to be delivered to people the very next day. Amazon forced many more companies, and not just those in directly competing categories, to ask a very challenging question: How can we match or top that level of convenience?

Remember: If your only reference point is yourself, it's all too easy to convince yourself that you're doing a great job.

When I hired Josy Paul to start up BBDO India in 2007, he had no office or staff but had to pitch for a huge account: 7Up, owned by PepsiCo. Josy, who previously ran an agency in India called David, said he wanted to start out with a completely clean slate before he set up an office or hired anyone. He thought it was important to get out into the world and understand what people in India were experiencing. He felt a strong need to forget the way he had done advertising in the past and listen instead to the future. He frequently traveled back and forth between Mumbai, where he lived, and Delhi, where Pepsi in India was based. Meeting lots of people in coffee shops was a good way to do that. He was also teaching creative development classes at St. Xavier's University in Mumbai, where he had received a physics degree. So he found it was most efficient for him to work out of his car, with a cellphone.

When you're in a coffee shop, often you or the person you're speaking with knows someone else there, and it can spark conversations you weren't expecting to have, Josy said.[6] "It's about your chemistry and how you invite people into the discussion." You're literally bringing new ideas to the table.

"Our advertising has to be interactive," Josy said. "It has to allow for conversations between the advertiser and the receiver. Every ad is a conversation." Josy feels that the nine months he spent without an office helped him deepen that conversation.

It was a major coup for BBDO India to land the account for 7Up. Shortly after Josy was hired, the head of marketing for 7Up wanted to meet with him in the BBDO offices, which did not yet exist. So Josy decided to say that the offices were being painted, so therefore could they meet at a coffee shop in the Taj Hotel. The marketing executive was happy to meet at this opulent hotel.

Before the meeting, Josy wrote some potential advertising scripts on cards and asked six of his students at St. Xavier's to accompany him to the meeting. When the head of marketing saw the students, she said, "My goodness, Josy, you have a very young team."

"Of course, because we're working with PepsiCo and 7Up, and it's a young brand and a young agency," Josy quickly said. Later, recounting the meeting, he added, "And these students in the coffee shop, they'd never done a presentation like this in their life. And she was very impressed."

THE RESONANCE OF RITUALS

In 2003 I was visiting Jim Kilts, who was CEO of Gillette at the time. He told me that, on average, people used a single razor blade for ten days. If only we could reduce that to just seven days, we could nearly double the profits of the company, he said.

The next morning, as I was shaving, I thought to myself: Why do I have such a clearly defined ritual for shaving every day, but I don't have one for changing my razor blade?

Soon after that I started changing my razor blade every week, making it a part of my Monday morning ritual. That got me to thinking about how powerful rituals are and led me to commission a study on them for BBDO, with the idea that a better grasp of rituals could lead to creative new products and campaigns—and even change people's behavior.

In our study we defined a ritual as "a transforming series of actions that help us enjoy passing from one emotional state to another."[7] Not only are they "a means of getting stuff done in the way that we prefer," but they are also an emotional journey.

It's important to understand rituals because, although they are created in the conscious mind, they pass quickly into the subconscious and so get repeated without much questioning. Because the motivation for rituals is often unconscious, you may not be able to get at them directly through market research or direct interviews.

What's the difference between a habit and a ritual? The distinction is that a habit is a deeply ingrained single behavior or set of behaviors, whereas a ritual is part of a pleasurable transformation into another emotional state. People can have bad habits, but we don't talk about having bad rituals. Rituals are harder to break because they're so embedded with personal meaning.

The study has by now become part of BBDO's DNA, said Melanie Norris, managing director and head of planning for BBDO Knows, based in London. It revealed "the absolute power and potential of rituals, not just to people and society, but to brands and their ability to grow and cement their position," she said in an interview.[8] The study was simple and elegant, and it revealed far more than anyone imagined it would, she said.

We talked to more than 6,000 people in twenty-eight countries as part of our quantitative and ethnographic study. Our research identified five main types of rituals, and we didn't realize how widespread they would turn out to be.

"These five things unite us regardless of culture, regardless of geography, regardless of age," Melanie said. Their universality makes them especially worthy of study. Consider how you might be able to use them in service of your next big creative idea:

Preparing for battle. This is the ritual that we perform from the time we wake up to the time we arrive at work or the place where we spend most of our day. It includes washing, eating/drinking, putting on clothes and makeup, and gathering information.

People perform an average of seven "preparing-for-battle" actions (the coffee/tea portion is especially cherished) before they leave home, we found. They prefer to perform these steps in the same order each day, using the same brands, and they become irritated and frustrated if those steps are disrupted, or if their preferred brand is not available. The tone of these rituals is "fast-paced, efficient and goal orientated."

The preparing-for-battle rituals help lighten a part of the day that can be fraught, painful, and full of friction, Melanie said, especially if you have children. They involve cramming the most steps into the smallest amount of time, and when much of people's behavior is on autopilot. This makes it a very difficult area to try to break into as a brand, "but once you're in, you're in," Melanie said.

Feasting. These rituals involve sharing food and include preparing, inviting, meeting, and contributing. Feasting "transforms us from feeling alone to being connected with our group." People tend to be more health- and efficiency-oriented with their feasting at the beginning of the week, and more adventurous, indulgent, and social at the end of the week and on weekends.

Sexing up. At its best, this is a confidence-giving ritual, filled with excitement and optimism. It "transforms us from our ordinary selves to our extraordinary or most special selves. . . . It includes cleansing, preparing, grooming, indulging, preening, and connecting with others."

And yet, ironically, this ritual can also fill us with anxiety, especially for women who feel pressure to look good and who worry that they won't measure up. Unlike the preparing-for-battle ritual, the sequence of actions for sexing up is not so important. But the details, such as the brands used, are critical.

Our understanding of this ritual has evolved and expanded since the original study was done, so that it now includes the idea of self-care and self-improvement.

Returning to camp. This is when we return home and—having separated ourselves from bosses, colleagues, other drivers on the highway, and subway and bus riders—to the comfort and choices of our true selves, in the privacy of our homes.

As our report noted, "We undo many of the things we did in the morning. Getting undressed. Almost everyone changes some item of clothing when they get home, be it taking off shoes, putting on joggers or a dressing gown. Taking off the makeup we put on 15 hours earlier. We eat. Perhaps as a group; perhaps in phases. We escape the pressure of the day through television, internet surfing, or idle conversation."

Locking up. These behaviors occur in the ten minutes before we turn in for the night and include literally locking doors and windows, along with unplugging things. They also include brushing your teeth, taking medications, pouring a glass of water to put on the nightstand (which more than half the people never actually drink, the study found), checking on children and pets, and setting out the items you need to prepare for battle the next day. "This ritual transforms us from relaxed to reassured."

The locking-up ritual is much slower and more considered, and can be more meaningful, than the preparing-for-battle ritual that starts the day, Melanie said. She has two children, and "the last thing I do is check on the kids before I shut the lights off." It's almost like a superstition, she added. "I cannot break that."

We urged our people to use the results of our study in three ways in particular:

Observe. We closely examine how people currently use our clients' products to assist with their rituals. Understanding that these behaviors can be incredibly powerful, we look for ways to break through "Fortress Ritual," as we call it. Weak points can emerge, for example, when someone runs out of a product, or moves, or travels to a foreign country. "Then we search for brand strengths that might encourage people to build a new ritual with our product inside it."

Interpret. "We're searching for the emotional purpose of the practical acts that are bound up in a particular ritual." Insightful interpretation of behavior that is so woven into people's lives—to the extent that it happens naturally almost every single day—has the potential to lead to powerful new creations with a wide-ranging impact.

Invent. "Creative ideas that are designed to embed a new ritual in our consumers' minds have a great deal more chance of success than a cool ad that's just sponsored entertainment." And once we have found our way inside Fortress Ritual, "our job is to pull up the drawbridge and keep rival brands out."

We sometimes suggest that companies use advertising to nudge people to move their rituals to a different part of the day, especially away from their action-crammed morning routine. For example, a health-care company encouraged people to use one of its over-the-counter products "every day." When people hear the words "every day," they take it to mean "every morning." Since the product was to help protect them from something bad that might happen in the future, it was much more likely to be included in the "locking-up" rituals at the end of the day than in the preparing-for-battle rituals of the morning. All the company had to do was change the wording from "use every day" to "use every night" (possibly with that glass of water on the nightstand they weren't using before!), and the brand stood a much better chance of having its use ritualized.

In another case, we found that people were using a certain brand of coffee once they finished their workouts in the afternoon, adding protein in it for an extra boost. This was a creative way for the company to increase sales outside of the crowded morning space, where people are very loyal to their coffee brands. These repositionings can result in big growth for a brand, Melanie said.

If a brand is determined to elbow its way into the crowded morning space, BBDO advises that it dial up its product's credentials about being a shortcut and removing pain. Vastly improved utility and functionality can be very emotionally fulfilling, Melanie said.

Breaking through Fortress Ritual often comes down to a basic question: What are you not seeing? It may turn out to be something that's hiding in plain sight.

The original study was done in 2007, but most of its findings still hold true today, Melanie said. People still engage in the five types of rituals, although the smartphone in particular has changed some of the ways those rituals play out. Many people now start the day gathering intelligence by looking at their phones. (We found that upon waking up, people often check their phones on the way to the bathroom, even before saying good morning to their partners.) And they now tend to end the day this way, too.

The pandemic also altered the way people performed the five rituals. For example, some people regularly took a walk before they started work and right afterward, to create a separation between waking up and preparing for battle, and between ending their workday and returning to camp. But the basic framework of the rituals remains intact.

THE IMPORTANCE OF EMPATHY

Going outside your usual surroundings and observing how customers interact with your brand "in the wild" is more likely to induce feelings of empathy for them in you. And empathy is an important component of creative thinking.

As David Kelley and Tom Kelley, of the renowned IDEO design firm, write in their book *Creative Confidence*, "In retail environments, we've discovered that if you change the question from 'how might we reduce customer waiting time?' to 'how might we reduce *perceived* customer waiting time?' it opens up whole new avenues of possibility, like using a video display wall to provide an entertaining distraction."[9] I'm sure it took someone sitting in a busy waiting room to understand how effective that "hack" would be.

Nothing fosters empathy more than putting yourself in the shoes of your end user and understanding what they really need, the Kelley brothers say. And it's hard to do that when you become totally walled off by things like your industry's professional jargon and specifications. It's too easy for customers "to become numbers, transactions, data points on a bell curve."[10]

One person who has made his fortune out of data parsing is Mark Zuckerberg, the CEO of Meta, owner of Facebook and other apps. But, especially after Facebook came under intense criticism for facilitating the spread of fake news and violent content, Zuckerberg felt that he needed to take some time to leave his "Silicon Valley bubble," as *The New York Times* reported.[11] In 2017, he embarked on a "Great American Road Trip" to gain a better sense of who the actual users of Facebook were. The trip brought him face to face with people he would never have met otherwise, including police officers, farmers, churchgoers, public school students, and recovering drug addicts.

"As I've traveled around, I've sat with children in juvenile detention and opioid addicts, who told me their lives could have turned out differently if they just had something to do, an after-school program or somewhere to go," Zuckerberg said in a commencement speech that year at Harvard (the school he dropped out of to start Facebook).[12] "I've met factory workers who know their old jobs aren't coming back and are trying to find their place."

Some critics said the trip was little more than a publicity stunt, but they don't know him. People close to Zuckerberg told the *Times* that it was a genuine effort on his part to better understand his audience. The trip, they said, "plunged him into self-reflection" over Facebook's role in society, and especially as a source of news and information.

Zuckerberg said that leaving the data-driven confines of Silicon Valley to tour America was one of the best things he had done. It gave him a sense of empathy that he had never had before.

As one academic paper on creativity put it, putting a new spin on a famous aphorism, "Empathy is the mother of invention."[13]

I would say that there's a step beyond empathy that makes a creative breakthrough even more likely, and more magical, and that is when deeply understanding your customers' perspective causes you to become truly fond of them.

My late colleague David Abbott used to talk about this. He told me, "One of the reasons I think the work I've done has landed the way it did, and has worked so well, is that I really like the audiences I'm writing for." When you put a barrier between yourself and your customers, and allow professional expertise and data reports to guide most of your work, the result is likely to be infected by cold rationalism. And that's no way to achieve magic.

CULTIVATE YOUR DOWNTIME

It's important to put your mind in idle mode from time to time.

About eight years ago, my wife strongly urged me to start meditating. She said, "I really think you need to do this because otherwise the stress of your job is going to kill you." I actually thought I was handling the stress pretty well, but I did agree to start meditating. Bob Roth, director of the David Lynch Foundation, which was founded by the film director to spread the practice of Transcendental Meditation, taught me how to do it.

Some people think that if you fail to achieve a perfectly blank and serene mind, you have somehow failed at meditation. But as Bob emphasized to us, there is no "good" or "bad" way to meditate. One of the key principles is that it's perfectly okay for your head to be filled with thoughts that come and go. That's just part of the brain processing everything that's been presented to it. Sometimes you might even fall asleep while meditating, and that's okay, too.

I like the analogy Bob makes to being in the ocean. As he wrote in his guide to Transcendental Meditation, *Strength in Stillness*, in the ocean "there are active, often turbulent waves on the surface, but there is calm at its depth."[14] The mind operates in a similar way: It is active on the surface, he writes, while "deep within is a level that is calm yet alert; silent yet wide awake. The ancient meditation texts refer to it as the 'source of thought' or 'pure consciousness'—a field of limitless creativity, intelligence, and energy within." This state of what scientists call "restful alertness" is always with us, he says. "The problem is, we have lost access to it."

I started meditating to relieve stress. And research shows that regular meditation massively reduces cortisol, the hormone that, when it goes into overdrive, is the source of most chronic stress. It's striking how many prominent creative types—Jerry Seinfeld, Sting, Paul McCartney, Lena Dunham, Oprah Winfrey, and Lady Gaga, to name just a few—practice Transcendental Meditation. They talk about using it to unblock mental obstacles and unlock creative insights.

I love doing the *New York Times* crossword, especially on Saturdays. I often get stuck, and I've found that if I go and meditate, when I come back I can solve six or seven clues that I hadn't been able to figure out before. It's not that I was consciously thinking about it while I was meditating, though; my mind was working on the clues subconsciously.

Walking is another way to nudge hidden creative ideas to the surface. Steve Jobs, for one, was famous for taking long walks and for bringing others with him for long walk-and-talks.

In a study titled "Give Your Ideas Some Legs," Marilyn Oppezzo and Daniel L. Schwartz of Stanford University reported the results of research showing that "whether one is outdoors or on a treadmill, walking improves the generation of novel yet appropriate ideas, and the effect even extends to when people sit down to do their creative work shortly after."[15]

Study participants took walks that lasted from five to sixteen minutes and were given tests that measured divergent thinking, a hallmark of creativity that involves exploring many possible solutions to problems. The researchers found that walking significantly increased divergent thinking, while having no effect on convergent thinking, which requires a more laser-like focus on a single problem or question.

"We're not saying walking can turn you into Michelangelo," Oppezzo said. "But it could help you at the beginning stages of creativity."

In one of the experiments, when participants were asked to come up with creative analogies in response to a prompt, "100 percent of those who walked outside were able to generate at least one high-quality, novel analogy"—for example, saying that a "robbed safe" could be compared to "a soldier suffering from PTSD." By contrast, only 50 percent of those seated inside were able to make a novel analogy (a noncreative answer to the "robbed safe" would be something like "an empty wallet").

People who pride themselves on their productivity can have a hard time allowing themselves to be idle, to let their minds wander. But numerous studies have shown that downtime is critical to creative thought.

People sometimes ask me if it's worth it to attend a certain conference. I respond that there are several possible benefits you can get out of a conference. One is that you might see a presentation from someone that is particularly inspirational or useful. But even if a presentation is as dull as ditchwater, you can still derive value from sitting in a dark room and not being able to do anything else for an hour, and letting your mind wander.

Similarly, I am often grateful when someone is late for a meeting with me, because it gives me a chance to just sit there with my random thoughts.

I used to enjoy the moment when I was settled in my airplane seat and the aircraft door closed, and, forcibly untethered from phone calls and emails, I was free to let my thoughts wander. Unfortunately, in-flight Wi-Fi has made those free-floating moments harder to achieve. Recently, though, a new trend known as flight "rawdogging" has gained some traction. This is where passengers deliberately abstain from any type of in-flight entertainment (with the more extreme practitioners denying themselves even food, water, and naps). The goal is to achieve mindfulness in the air.[16]

I make it a point to tell my people that taking a break for creativity's sake is part of their job. This is a different kind of break from the kind you take to relax and recharge. Those breaks are important too, of course. But I also need my people to intentionally stop toggling between emails, calling up files, and checking the next thing off their list and simply clear their brains. However they choose to do it—by listening to Mozart on their headphones, taking a walk in Central Park, or something else—I'm reasonably sure that their "idleness" will yield creative dividends later on. It's all part of the creative process.

Now there's a limit to this. There's not working and then there's shirking. The proof shows up in someone's ideas—or lack of them. If someone is taking regular walks in the park and is consistently contributing brilliant ideas, then that's a sign that they are using their downtime wisely. If they're wandering the park for two hours a day and not making any creative contributions, then that's just walking in the park. And sooner or later, they'll be walking the plank.

The concept of "working while you're not working" can be hard for CEOs and managers of precision-based, operationally excellent companies to wrap their minds around. But they need to embrace this concept if they want to achieve a Creative Shift.

I know that by encouraging my people to engage with the outside world, to interact directly with clients and consumers, and to let their minds wander, their work is likely to be orders of magnitude better than if they hadn't done those things. If I tell them about a big challenge we face or a major new foundational campaign we need to plan, I know their brains will start to engage with it, whether they're aware of it or not.

But it's important to understand that most people would be happy to languish indefinitely in a warm bath of vague and partially formed ideas. Most people need structure and deadlines and the stimulating company of others in order to fully actualize their creative thinking. That's what our WorkOuts are for.

ACTIVATE
YOUR SPACE

I know from personal experience that when it comes to cre-ativity, the space you occupy and the way it is arranged both matter a great deal. But too many companies act on that principle only superficially, without really thinking through the how and the why of what they're doing.

In the 1960s, organizations encouraged creativity through decor. Cutting-edge corporate research centers like Xerox PARC put weird chairs in architecturally striking spaces intentionally designed to encourage serendipitous encounters.

Though it's faded since its heyday, this trend never com-pletely went away. Ad agencies, for one, have always been fond of unconventional interior design to signal, if not actually encourage, creativity: from artificial-turf walls to strategically placed piles of LEGO blocks. Tech companies also go in for quirky signals: "The aquariums mean we think differently here."

(Actually, fish are meant to relax people, not stir them up creatively, which is why you sometimes see them in doctor's and dentist's offices. David Abbott, who could have been a stand-up comedian if he hadn't pursued advertising, used this fact to his sardonic advantage when we moved to new offices in London. He noted in a celebratory speech that his partner Peter Mead's new office had a fish tank, which he said would be great for the fish because they could relax as they watched him work.)

But is quirkiness the signal your company wants to send? Customers, clients, and vendors often seek certainty, discipline, efficiency, and compliance. Who wants to trust their life savings to a bank with tables made out of LEGO blocks?

Likewise, calling something a creative space doesn't make it so. For example, a major bank renamed its conference rooms "Imagine," "Create," and "Explore," yet as far as I could tell had done nothing to change its approach to imagining, creating, or exploring. I recall going to the offices there for a pitch and asking the receptionist in the lobby, "I'm sorry to bother you, but could you please direct me to Urinate?" She didn't so much as smile before directing me to the washroom, and we didn't get the business (I'm not sure if there was a correlation).

DESIGNING CREATIVE HABITATS

Putting careful thought into the design of your offices—and offering different spaces for different types of thinking and working—will yield exponential benefits when you bring your people together for brainstorming sessions. Some offices are much better seedbeds for creativity than others.

The debate goes back and forth on open-plan vs. closed offices. There's no question that open-plan offices can get in the way of single-minded focus. Hearing the random chats, phone calls, text pings, munches, crunches, and sniffles of your colleagues can be very distracting and annoying. There's a reason why noise-canceling headphones were invented—and why it's wise to have quieter spaces available for really deep thinking. Because they work so well, I'm a fan of the open-plan office, however, especially as it relates to creativity. When it comes to generating ideas, density is your ally.

One reason for this is that it promotes eavesdropping. Research has shown that overhearing the conversations of others can have multiple benefits. It can help you better gauge the emotions of coworkers, so, for example, you can decide not to raise a difficult issue when you know someone is already in a sour mood. And it can give you a better understanding of your company's culture and unofficial power structure, and how best to operate and make changes within it.

I would say that eavesdropping also enlarges an organization's creativity zone, by increasing the number of connections between people and the way those connections are formed. It's similar to the way synaptic connections and neural pathways expand in the creative brain. These little gems of overheard information enter into your conscious and unconscious mind in a different way than the inputs that directly affect your work.

Now, I'm not saying you should lean in closer when a colleague is talking in a low tone with her doctor about the results of her colonoscopy, or when another colleague is engaged in a bitter, under-the-breath marital dispute. Of course you should ignore—or at least pretend to ignore—those conversations. But if eavesdropping helps you better understand someone else's job or gives you tips on how to perform your own job better, then why not make use of it?

In fact, design firms are creating office spaces that actively encourage eavesdropping; it's an overt recognition that people can learn from each other and gather valuable intelligence that way. In particular, employers see these types of arrangements as a way for junior employees to learn from more senior ones, according to a recent article in *The Wall Street Journal*.[1]

The design firm Gensler has been developing more workspaces to allow for "a spectrum of acoustic privacy," Brian Stromquist, who leads the technology practice at the firm, said in the article. One part of the office may be open plan, to permit conversations to be overheard, while other areas may use white noise or music to drown out voices, and still other spaces are specifically designated for deep focusing.

THE DRAWBACKS OF REMOTE WORK

This is yet another reason that I regret the rise of remote work. I believe that in so many ways physical proximity is key to creative collaboration. Being in the same physical space as others allows you to draw on the energy of others when your own starts flagging. That energy just doesn't exist on a screen.

I'm a SoulCycle addict, having done almost 2,000 rides, most of them in a studio and many fewer of them at home. You might think that riding at home would be pretty similar to riding in the studio, especially if you have the same instructor. But I've found that it's not nearly as invigorating, because you aren't giving and getting energy from other people. The same applies to a Zoom or Teams or Google Meet screen.

Of course, we made do with remote work during the worst of the pandemic, but I saw the negative effect that it had.

Video conferences are fine for updates and process-oriented discussions, but they tend to have a stifling effect on collaboration. The only way you can run a video meeting with, say, twelve people is to put someone in charge who invites people to speak when they put their hand up. And that's just not how things happen in real life. Even when there's a designated facilitator at an in-person meeting, people can jump in with interjections and indicate with their body language how they feel about an idea. You can literally feel the heat in the room. A trail of thumbs-up and heart emojis on a screen is nothing like one person leaping up and exclaiming, "Oh my god, I love that!"

I've participated in a few meetings in Horizon Workrooms, created by Meta, and they are definitely an improvement over flat-screen video meetings—once you get used to working with avatars that have no legs. And I got used to it far more quickly than I imagined I would.

In the metaverse, after you've created your own avatar, you put on a headset and interact with other avatars in a 3D virtual space. Facial expressions like the raising of an eyebrow or a smile or a frown are replicated in real time on your avatar. What's especially great about Horizon is that when someone speaks, you actually turn your head to look at them. It makes you realize how important not just words, but sounds, are to the way we interact and collaborate.

Yes, the technology is improving, but nothing will ever replace the creative energy of real-life collaboration. That's why I regret, while fully understanding, the preference people developed for working from home as a result of the pandemic.

You can make all of the following arguments to your people about coming into the office:

1. We do better work when we're together.
2. We do the work faster.
3. It's more fun and energizing when we're in the same space.
4. We learn more in an office by watching, listening to, and overhearing others.
5. Our culture is easier to build and nurture when people are physically together.

Yes, people will agree wholeheartedly with all these things, but when you ask why it wouldn't then make sense for everyone to return to the office full time, most will still say something along the lines of, "Because I don't want to." It is as irritatingly illogical as the answer of a parent who is tired of being asked "why?" by a toddler: "Because I say so."

There are many advantages to working from home. In recognition of that, after the pandemic many companies said their people could start coming in three days a week instead of five. The problem with coming in three days a week, though, is that it isn't enough to solidify a routine, and people need routine to feel truly comfortable in the work they do. As I noted before, people establish rituals around their work routines, and when they're constantly switching between home and the office to work, the conscious mental effort required to go from one to the other adds a layer of cognitive stress and exhaustion that can inhibit productivity—and creativity.

Simon Vicars, our brilliant chief creative officer in New Zealand, did something smart: After the worst of the pandemic, he got his people together and said, "For three months we're all going to come into the office every day, and after that we'll decide what to do going forward." He understood that what people wanted right then, after being in the cocoon of working from home after a deadly pandemic, might well be different from what they wanted in the future.

After the three months, people were happy with their revived work routine, and there was no big push to change it.

AN UNFAMILIAR SPACE

One thing I will never give up on: the importance of moving people to a different space altogether to generate ideas. This has a remarkable effect on creative thinking, whether you're dreaming up a new product or mapping out next year's sales strategy. It's also an effective team-building tool.

Above all, it sends a strong message: This is a different realm from your day-to-day space. One where you can feel free—where indeed you will be encouraged—to be wild, wacky, and just plain wrong.

I don't think a certain type of space can inspire creativity on its own, but it can at least remove the obstacles that normally get in the way of it. If you have the time and can afford to hold an offsite, it should generally be in a place that's fairly easy for your people to get to, so they don't spend half a day traveling each way.

And try to avoid a big conference hotel with cavernous boring meeting rooms if you can. There's a cookie-cutter symbolism that tends to pervade these hotels. A boutique hotel or a mansion or art gallery or some type of funky event space is a better choice. (I've often thought that a primary school would be a great place for a WorkOut. On the one hand, it might help people get in touch with their inner child. On the other hand, the tiny chairs might be too uncomfortable.)

Even if you don't have the time or the resources to go offsite, you can still hold a WorkOut. (See my suggestions for a "Diet WorkOut" in Chapter 5.) You just need to keep the following elements in mind:

The room. The room should not be too big or too small. It should have enough space for about a dozen people to move around in comfortably—after you remove the conference table, if there is one (see below on the importance of doing that). And there should be plenty of wall space for hanging giant paper easels (again, see below).

The walls. There needs to be plenty of empty wall space in the collaboration room, or, in a pinch, window space. Huge heavy original artworks that hang from the walls are not an advantage in this case.

The air. Make sure you have good temperature control, and someone who is charge of it, for your WorkOut. You want to start out on the warmer side, but then dial it down as people start to get up and move around and heat up with ideas.

The chairs. When you're preparing for a Creative Shift, it's very important to have the right chairs. The chairs should be comfortable but not too comfortable. You don't want a stiff wooden chair that causes people to start rubbing their shoulders, necks, and backs. But you also don't want to bring in a load of bean bags that cause people to loll in them until they fall asleep.

And this is very important: The chairs need to be lightweight so you can pick them up and move them around and put them in different groupings—similar to how the ideas generated by the people in those chairs will be configured and reconfigured.

There's a famous *New Yorker* cover from 1976 by Saul Steinberg called "View of the World from 9th Ave" that I have hanging in my Manhattan office. It shows a few blocks of Manhattan as being the center of the world. Just a few states and only five other cities are peripherally included. Canada and Mexico, along with the Pacific Ocean, Japan, China, and Russia, are represented way off in the distance. Europe, Africa, and South America are not even shown. For me, the poster is a reminder that the world appears the way it does because of where you're sitting, and that the best way to change your perspective is to move your seat.

Moving chairs during a collaborative session is a simple way to prod people to look at things from varying perspectives and help them to understand in a visceral way that their viewpoint is far from the only one.

A big table? No! People tend to think of brainstorming as occurring at a big conference table, but I have found that conference tables are a great way for people to hide and protect themselves. It is also very hard to change your position if you are sitting at a big long table. You want people to be open and flexible and mobile at these creative sessions. So ditch the conference table.

The paper. I swear, 3M is not a client of ours, and I don't mean for this book to be an advertisement for them, but the fact is, they make those giant paper easels that you can stick on a wall so as to cover them with the Post-it notes that they also make. (And be sure to get some little round stickers, too, for evaluating all the ideas on the Post-its.)

Please do *not* use a whiteboard for these exercises. Whiteboards are great for straightforward planning and processes, but they are idea killers—literally—in the sense that you can rub them out with the swipe of an eraser. You want all the ideas that people suggest to stay alive until the evaluation stage.

Maybe one idea on a Post-it doesn't work on one of the easels, but you realize it could be good friends with a group of Post-its on another easel. So you walk it over to that other easel. Not possible with a whiteboard.

And it's nice to know that even after you have rolled up one of the white easel papers and thrown it in the garbage, you still have the opportunity to retrieve it.

The food. Have good and nutritious food available, just outside the room. Keeping food inside the room can be disruptive. Also, keeping food separate gives people a good reason to leave the room to take a mental break. And whatever you do, don't serve pizza (or shrimp), as these can leave an unpleasant smell long after they are served.

When an offsite isn't feasible, you can change things up in other ways. This can be as simple as asking colleagues to join you for a walk-and-talk instead of sitting around a conference table, or orienting your desk in a different direction.

At BBDO we have three main types of spaces for gathering people together. One is a collaborative space, such as the type we use at our WorkOuts, where we have flexible chairs, plenty of empty space, and no tables. Then there are the rooms where we hold meetings to discuss updates and process and timelines, things like that. You do want tables for these types of gatherings, although I am a big fan of having high tables that force people to stand, because the meetings tend to be shorter. Then we have our presentation rooms, which are not used as often as the other rooms but are nevertheless extremely important as a way to convince people of the brilliance of our ideas and usher them through to the execution stage.

THE BBDO ASHRAM

Josy Paul, head of our offices in India, is a big believer in the power of workspaces to create different impressions and stimulate different kinds of creative thought. As I mentioned earlier, when he ran his upstart agency David (a reference to David vs. Goliath), he set up his offices as a colorful, toy-filled playschool where people had to sign a paper agreeing to resign from adulthood before coming inside.

And in the first nine months of running BBDO India, he operated the agency out of the back seat of his car, which he chose to do so he would be forced to go out into the world and meet as many people as he could in coffee shops.

Then, while he and his agency partner, Ajai Jhala, were working out of a small coworking space, they took a trip to Ahmedabad, in the Gujarat region, to try to win new business. Their meeting was in the morning, and the flight back to Mumbai was in the evening, so during their six free hours, Josy suggested that they visit Gandhi's ashram, which he knew was nearby and had always wanted to see.

Gandhi had lived at the ashram from 1917 to 1930, with the purpose of carrying on "a search for truth and a platform to bring together a group of workers committed to nonviolence who would help secure freedom for India," as the ashram's website explains.[2]

"They've done a beautiful job of telling the stories of the movement, and it was like an epiphany for us when we went there," Josy recalled.[3] "Just being there and touching history and knowing that a nation was born there can affect you. This is where India's freedom began. This is where the struggle started."

On the flight back, Josy said to Ajai, "I think I have a one-word brief for the people who are going to do the interiors for our empty space: ashram. The minute we say the word ashram it will create a new vibe."

For the BBDO Ashram (that is literally what it is called and what the sign outside the office says), the architects used the same types of materials that Gandhi did. Josy recalled, "I said, 'For me Gandhi is our creative director.' Let's put his symbols everywhere so everyone understands."

The symbols include a simple wooden *charkha*, a spinning wheel that was used on the flag of the Provisional Government of Free India in 1921. Gandhi invoked (and literally used) the charkha as a way to encourage Indians to rely on their own industries—like weaving—rather than remaining financially dependent on the British government.

I wrote earlier about the importance of using signals to evoke organizational culture, and I think Josy's ashram does this very powerfully. He says he wants his ashram to symbolize that "we are not a hierarchy—we have to work as a collective and use the power of our collective to believe in each other" and in our ability to do great things. "People need symbols they can look at and feel and say, 'I'm a part of this.'"

Initially, Josy wanted to create an overhead light that kept moving so the spotlight would be on everyone at one time or another. That was not really feasible, he said, but he still likes the idea behind it. "Conceptually I was trying to say that everyone was important."

Inspired by Gandhi, Josy became convinced that "every business that we handle has a powerful cause within it and we can find it." Gandhi also believed in the cumulative power of small individual actions. Josy thought, "If we can create a small action for our brands, then more people can be part of that action. Create *acts*, not ads. Because the more acts you can create, the more people will be engaged with the product."

Because of this philosophy, BBDO India has played a significant role in shining a light on women's issues. One example is its "Touch the Pickle" campaign, which won a Cannes Lions Award in 2015. Created to sell Whisper sanitary pads made by Procter & Gamble, the ads literally started a movement to break deeply entrenched taboos that forbid menstruating women from performing a range of activities that include worshipping, playing sports, and entering the kitchen. Even touching a jar of pickles (a widely used seasoning in India) was considered off-limits in the belief that it would cause the pickles to go bad.

"I say, girls, let's go ahead and break the taboo," says a girl in one of the TV ads. It encouraged others to join the #touchthepickle movement. Soon, women were posting photos of themselves on Facebook, Instagram, and other social media sites daring to touch the pickle jar during their periods. As Business Insider said, "Not only did 2.9 million pledge to touch the pickle jar, but the work resulted in sparking a huge conversation in India around the issue."[4]

And BBDO India's "Share the Load" ads, for P&G's Ariel laundry detergent, addressed the inequity of women being expected to handle the lion's share of the housework in addition to working outside the home. In one commercial, an older man is disturbed by a growing distance between him and his wife and has a heart-to-heart talk with his daughter about it as they're driving to a movie.

"I've been thinking . . . could it be something I did?" the man asks his daughter.

She answers, "Papa, you know I love you both equally. . . . May I say something? Mama's just been giving and giving for so long [cut to scenes of Mama doing housework while Papa talks on the phone and looks at his computer]. I'm afraid that she's just given up."

The man suddenly realizes that he's been taking his wife for granted and asks his daughter to take him back home. We see his exhausted wife sleeping on the couch and then waking up to the sound of the washing machine. As she rises, her husband approaches her with a cup of coffee.

"I'm sorry," he says to the amazed woman, who must be wondering if she's dreaming.

"Can we start again?" says the man.

He then proceeds to take the laundry out of the machine—after having used Ariel laundry detergent to clean it, of course.

Then, on the screen: "Are you growing together or growing apart? Share the load."

In another project for Procter & Gamble, this one for Gillette razors, BBDO India started a tongue-and-cheek movement called "Women Against Lazy Stubble." The ads capitalized on a survey showing that (gorgeous movie stars with sexy stubble notwithstanding) most women prefer their men to be clean-shaven. The ads were so influential that a group of men started a group called Men Against Women Against Lazy Indian Stubble, who argued that the ads amounted to a violation of men's rights.

"Share the Load," "Women Against Lazy Stubble," and "Touch the Pickle" were named as three of the most iconic ad campaigns of the decade at the Cannes Lions Network and Marketer of the Decade Awards in 2020. And the spirit and symbols of the ashram space enabled those ads to come into being, Josy said.

A lot of these ideas first surfaced in the ashram's "white room," which is all white and where people sit on cushions and talk to each other, sometimes about very personal memories and experiences. This is not a room for brainstorming, but rather for "soul-storming," Josy said. When you're brainstorming, you can't help but want to be, or at least seem to be, clever, he said. But when you're soul-storming, you're listening, and asking questions, and confessing. There is no moderator, and so everyone is equal, with no hierarchy. This is a room that encourages people to go deeper, and, as Josy noted, "maybe from that can come new ideas that have depth."

"Every year we discover something new through soul-storming," he said. In the white room, "it's not so much about insights as it is about confessions. Insights give you truths, which is great, but confessions give you deeper truths. The white room is a monument to the deeper truths that we seek."

And once all those ideas and confessions emerge, you need to find a way to catch the deepest and most meaningful ones in the service of your creative goals.

CHAPTER 9

CATCHING IDEAS

It's All About the Fish

Alex Osborn, one of the founders of BBDO and the father of brainstorming, said, "If you go fishing you may not catch any fish. If you don't go fishing, you'll never catch any fish."

And the film director David Lynch said, "Ideas are like fish. If you want to catch little fish, you can stay in the shallow water. But if you want to catch the big fish, you've got to go deeper. Down deep, the fish are more powerful and more pure."[1]

To catch ideas in your organization, you need to actively go fishing for them—and cast a *very* wide net. I estimate that you'll throw at least 90 percent of those fish back into the water, and that's okay. Because the 10 percent that you keep—and that you never would have caught otherwise—will make the whole effort supremely worthwhile.

Think of all the ideas that swim around, consciously or unconsciously, in your own brain. Now multiply that by the ideas harbored by all your colleagues. As a leader, if you can find an effective way to surface and combine, winnow and refine, all those ideas, the result in creative thinking will be enormous.

Business leaders always need to balance today's needs against tomorrow's possibilities, constantly thinking of how to stay ahead of the competition: new products, services, and improvements to every aspect of customer experience. Building an intentional habit of creativity throughout your organization is crucial if you want ideas to arrive before it's too late to use them.

Preparing and planning for a Creative Shift needs to be part of your structure, your culture, and your routine, so that you are primed to take advantage of all that potential when you need to come up with the truly big idea. No one gets good ideas when doom feels imminent. When leaders declare, "Innovate, or we're screwed," usually everyone just freezes.

People need time and a sense of security to explore, observe, and ponder possibilities without worrying about tight deadlines and punitive consequences. From spending a few minutes jotting down ideas each day to engaging in weekly meetings with the team so that everyone can share their latest thinking about the road ahead, creativity deserves its share of every schedule *before* a crisis arises.

And it starts at the top, with leaders making it a point to proclaim creativity as a cultural value. In part, this means conveying, through concrete signals and rewards, that leaders believe *all* their people are creative, and that contributing ideas is valued—whether the ideas are good or bad, whether they end up being used or not.

Just about all leaders like to think they truly listen to their people. But it takes real effort to create an environment where all suggestions are created equal. Because in a typical organizational hierarchy they most definitely are not.

"Far too often, employees willfully choose to self-censor out of a fear of negative repercussions to their career or social standing," according to researchers David A. Hofmann and John J. Sumanth, writing in the *Harvard Business Review.*[2] "Yet, when employees do choose to speak up, research suggests that a host of positive things can happen, including higher engagement and job satisfaction, greater learning, enhanced innovations and creativity, fewer accidents and safer workplaces, and even better unit financial performance."

With such a wealth of benefits tied to ideas from everywhere, how do organizations remove the very real fears that prevent them from emerging?

For one thing, leaders must acknowledge that they don't have all the answers, the researchers wrote. "Your focus should be on *accomplishing* the goal, not *advocating* for your particular idea about how best to achieve it. Yet, for many leaders, relinquishing commitment to their own solutions and ideas is difficult, particularly for those who are insecure about their own abilities or view their followers as a potential threat to their position or status in the organization."

I remember much earlier in my career working with an executive at a large cereal company. He was one of the most frightening businesspeople I've ever met. At a meeting he actually told one of his people who dared to express a point of view, "When I want your opinion, I'll tell you what it is." We've probably all worked with people who operate under this principle, whether they say it out loud or not.

WHAT DO THEY REALLY THINK?

When Sainsbury's was our client in the 1990s, it was standard practice for all of their most senior management to go on weekly store visits, always on a Friday. An executive would arrive at a given store in a chauffeur-driven car (often a Jaguar) at a predefined and well-shared time, and as he walked in (at the time, it unfortunately was always a he), you could tell that the store manager had to resist the urge to give him a full military salute. A surprise visit this was not. Nor could it be classified as "walking in your customers' shoes."

The executive would proceed to have a perfunctory conversation with a shopper and maybe a cashier or someone who was stocking the shelves. A few of these executives managed to glean some insights from these highly artificial situations, but most were not really trying to learn anything—although, as the chauffeur opened the back door of the Jaguar for them, they perhaps convinced themselves that they had.

I'm pretty sure that no one at BBDO feels the urge to salute me, but I'm aware that people are unlikely to be completely comfortable and candid with me in traditional business settings. I know I have to overcompensate for that if I want to hear what people really think.

When I travel to other BBDO offices, I try my best to make it not seem like a royal visit. Sometimes I do need to give presentations, and receive them, but I also like to just sit in an office and work on something while other people do their work, too. In time, I find that people forget about my title and position, and I'm able to participate naturally in conversations, ask questions, and pick up valuable information and ideas.

I can assure you that this way of working yields huge creative dividends. As does talking individually with a diverse mix of people who work with you. I never summon someone to my office for these informal chats. I prefer to meet and talk where they are. And I make sure they know that I'm there to listen and learn, not to tell.

I'm also a big fan of the walk-and-talk (hey, it worked for Steve Jobs). One of my most effective executives used to walk with me from my office to the elevator. He got more out of me in those few minutes than others did in hours of meetings.

Of course, it's not realistic to think that leaders are going to be able to capture all their people's ideas through one-on-one conversations. So how do you gather and collate the ideas that are swirling about in the minds of your people before they disappear? We do it very efficiently through our Work-Outs, but there are other ways to surface ideas too.

Organizations have long utilized the humble suggestion box as a way of soliciting ideas. Recently the physical boxes have evolved into actual idea-management software. Make it easy for someone to fill out an electronic form with an idea, the thinking goes, and you may well find the foundational nugget for your next big breakthrough.

That's the goal, anyway. But it generally doesn't work out that way. In fact, just asking for vague suggestions is a surefire way to generate a litany of far-flung complaints. I think suggestion boxes or portals are a terrible idea because of their open-endedness. (It's similar to what happens when you gather people around a table for brainstorming and say, How can we be more creative? Not much.) If you ask for *ideas* about a particular *issue*, you are much more likely to receive worthwhile insights.

It's better to spend time on devising a specific question or challenge, the way Patricia Corsi—now chief growth officer at Kimberly-Clark—did when she headed marketing at Heineken in Mexico. As I described in Chapter 5, she sponsored monthly creative contests, with rewards, designed to spur people to come up with solutions for specific challenges. These resulted in some ingenious ideas, including one from someone in the procurement department who suggested a way to recycle residues from beer-making into material that could be used in manufacturing plastic cups given out at festivals.

WHAT'S IN YOUR DRAWER?

Legend has it that the artist James McNeill Whistler and the writer Oscar Wilde were speaking at a party when Whistler made a very witty remark. Oscar Wilde immediately said, "I wish I had said that," and Whistler responded, "You will, Oscar, you will." The point being that successful ideas (and witticisms) often end up having many parents. But what about the ideas that aren't an immediate success?

Have you ever had a wonderful, creative idea, and wanted to share it with someone, but feared that it would be rejected? Or maybe you *did* show it to someone and it *was* rejected. But still, you knew the idea had value. Maybe you didn't quite know how, or when, or for whom.

Patricia knows that feeling. When she was a marketing executive at Unilever, she started a program called Creative Unleashed to harness it.

She got the idea for Creative Unleashed when she was in a London meeting with an ad agency and one of the creative directors took her aside and asked, a little nervously, if he could show her something confidentially. She was afraid it would be some kind of complaint. Instead, he said, "I have a couple of ideas that I think are marvelous, but the team doesn't like them. Can I show them to you? And if you don't like them, then I'll just put them back in the drawer."[3]

"And I said: 'What drawer?'" Patricia recalled recently. And he said: I have a drawer where I keep all of my ideas that the clients have rejected. And Patricia said, "Open the drawer."

What came out of the drawer was a simple but gorgeous print ad that Patricia ended up using for Colman's mustard and that won a Lion in Cannes.

"So then I said, 'I will never stop asking to see the drawer,'" Patricia recalled.

For some it's a metaphorical drawer in, say, a folder on a computer desktop. For others it's a literal drawer in a file cabinet. Wherever it is, it represents one or more ideas that shouldn't have been rejected in the first place, or weren't the right idea for that particular product, or were the right idea at the wrong time.

Patricia has transferred her Creative Unleashed program to other companies she has joined, including Heineken and Bayer. She has been able to carve out a small portion of her marketing budget for her unconventional approach and has full decision rights over that small pot of money.

Since starting her program, Patricia has found that 50 percent of the ideas from the drawer are "pure gold," while another 30 percent are good ideas that could use some improvement before turning into gold. Pretty good odds for ideas that probably would have stayed forever buried otherwise.

Patricia has invited ad agencies like ours not only to search through drawers but also to develop and present ideas for Creative Unleashed. It's not at all like the usual process, because there's no brief from the client, and no testing. Patricia uses her gut to make the final decision on whether to proceed with an idea. "It's all about boldness," she said. "If all the ideas presented are good and safe, it's not going to work."

It was through the Creative Unleashed process that Bayer launched a campaign around something it created called the Vagina Academy, aimed at marketing a product called Canesten to treat yeast infections.

The campaign began in Brazil, where Patricia was born and raised, and where any discussion of one's private parts tends to be highly taboo. She discovered that most women in Brazil were too afraid even to say the word "vagina" to their gynecologist, and that they did not want to be seen going near the Canesten shelf in the store.

Normalize the word "vagina": That was the idea that came out of a Creative Unleashed session. Running with the idea, Patricia and her team set up tens of thousands of educational sessions for Brazilian women at the Vagina Academy, meant to provide information on and raise awareness about women's gynecological conditions. The campaign was a big success and expanded into twelve countries worldwide.

Part of what makes Creative Unleashed work, Patricia said, is that she takes full accountability for the results. She tells the CEO, "I'm doing this, and if it doesn't work, then you can fire me. No one else. Because I'm making those decisions."

Although there is no brief from the client, that doesn't mean the ad agencies don't work with one. It just means that the defined question comes from us rather than from the client. When we present the answer, it's to a question the client hasn't asked.

Creative Unleashed is a great example of starting at the end and giving someone an answer first. When the meetings take place, you present a finished idea as opposed to engaging in the linear process of moving point by point from problem to solution.

This is a completely self-contained exercise where the normal rules around pitching an idea no longer apply. It's sheer inspiration and brilliance that bring the best ideas to the fore. And I've found that that serves to raise everyone's game—not just in the ads that emerge from Creative Unleashed, but in the work that agencies do as part of annual marketing plans as well.

The free-wheeling, unconstrained style of Creative Unleashed led us to propose an ad campaign for a Bayer brand when Patricia worked there. It involved highlighting a problem that just about every worker experiences but rarely talks about: the embarrassment inherent in using shared restrooms.

Our unconventional pitch led to the 2022 #workstipation campaign, which was perfect for people returning to work after the worst of the pandemic. It was also a great fit for MiraLAX, the laxative Bayer markets.

"After a year of doing our business in the comfort of our homes, we're about to face one harsh reality about going back to the office that MiraLAX wants to change," the announcer deadpans as music worthy of a superhero movie plays in the background amid scenes of shared office restrooms. "Workstipation: the stress of going at the office with a backed-up gut."

In the tone of someone reading a manifesto, the announcer asserts that workers deserve the right to "unpeekable" stalls—to go incognito, and without coworkers right outside their stall. "We deserve a stress-free place to free our guts!" the announcer proclaims.

I can confidently say that these ads would never have seen the light of day if not for the Creative Unleashed program.

AN IDEA FINDS ITS TIME AND PLACE

If Spencer Silver, a chemist, had been working for a different company, it's possible that the germ of a brilliant idea he had would have disintegrated inside a metaphorical drawer. Fortunately, Silver worked for 3M, which has long supported a culture of surfacing and nurturing creative ideas over time.

In 1968, Silver was a 3M chemist on a quest to develop a new adhesive that would be strong enough for use in aircraft construction. While experimenting with various chemicals, he developed an acrylic adhesive that was of no use whatsoever for building aircraft because it was so weak.

A normal person at a normal company might have viewed the not-very-sticky material as just another failed experiment. Not Silver. He was convinced it was a breakthrough, so he eventually patented the material, and he was relentless about finding a use for it—so much so that he was known throughout the company as "Mr. Persistent." He gave regular seminars on the adhesive and even distributed samples of it throughout the company.

It took a while, but the spark was finally ignited in the mid-1970s. A 3M chemical engineer named Art Fry heard about the material from a colleague while playing on 3M's corporate golf course and decided to attend one of Silver's seminars.

Fry already knew Silver, but not well. "We had crossed paths in things like the bicycle club," he recalled in Silver's *New York Times* obituary in 2021.[4] "3M always devised ways to mix people from different divisions."

At first Fry couldn't think of a use for this "solution to a problem that did not appear to exist" either. But then, when he was singing in his church's choir, he started to use the adhesive as a bookmark in his hymnal. It was perfect for that purpose, because it was sticky enough to stay put but could also be easily removed without tearing the pages or leaving any residue behind.

The two men tested the improved version on 3M employees, who used the paper adhesives for notes and reminders. "I thought what we have here isn't just a bookmark," Fry told CNN in 2013. "It's a whole new way to communicate."[5]

The product was finally launched in 1980. "The Post-it notes took off so rapidly that I think it left a lot of people in marketing and sales gasping a little bit," Silver told CNN.

In the realm of office supplies, the Post-it is surely one of the greatest inventions of the twentieth century. Because of the Creative Shift that Silver and Fry achieved, we at BBDO are able to achieve Creative Shifts of our own in our WorkOuts. Sticking those big paper easels on the wall, covering them with Post-its, and removing some of those Post-its and walking them across the room to another easel— Post-it adhesives enable us to mix and match ideas with ease. When I'm visiting high-tech companies like Meta, I am often struck by how even the people there make frequent use of them.

The Post-it note is an example of a novel idea that came to fruition not only because of Silver and Fry's persistence, but also because of a culture of creativity that was embedded within 3M.

As Silver was quoted saying in a 3M anniversary publication, "Thomas Edison believed that a small group of people with varied backgrounds could be the most inventive."[6] At 3M, he "could talk to an analytical chemist, a physicist, people working in biology and organic chemistry—people in all the sciences. They were all within 50 yards."

Note that 3M also created a variety of ways for people to meet outside the office, such as on the golf course and in the bicycle club, with the idea that interactions in those milieus might just lead to unexpected connections between people and new ideas.

And even though some executives were skeptical of the adhesive's utility, 3M allowed Fry and Silver to continue improving it through the company's "bootlegging" program, which encourages people to devote up to 15 percent of their work time to pet projects.

"The leaders of 3M understood that no one should stand in the way of a creative person with passion because that person might invent the next product or manufacturing breakthrough," according to the anniversary publication.

Bootlegging has been a permitted practice at the company almost since it was founded at the turn of the twentieth century. It proved its worth when an engineering school dropout and former professional banjo player named Dick Drew secretly continued to work on an adhesive that would make car painting easier, even after his boss ordered him to stop and switch to a different project.

The "forbidden" project that Drew refused to give up turned into Scotch masking tape in 1925, which later evolved into Scotch cellophane tape, introduced in 1930. As the anniversary publication explained, those successes helped to lead 3M executives to support "the idea that technical people could disagree with management, experiment, and do some fooling around on their own."

The encouragement of bootlegging encourages people to nurture hunches over time, and to await the right combination of forces to make their ideas a reality.

THE POWER OF ASKING FOR HELP

Another thing 3M has done is cultivate a culture of *helping*. The people there are actively encouraged to lend their expertise to others both inside and outside their departments, and to seek help from others.

An article in the *Harvard Business Review* talks about the importance of "making collaborative generosity the norm" as a way to spur organizational creativity.[7] This kind of "citizenship behavior" in organizations is especially important "when positive business outcomes depend on creativity in often very complex projects," say the authors, Teresa Amabile, Colin Fisher, and Julianna Pillemer.

"Helpfulness must be actively nurtured in organizations, however, because it does not arise automatically among colleagues," the authors note. "Individuals in social groups experience conflicting impulses. As potential helpers, they may also be inclined to compete. As potential help seekers, they may also take pride in going it alone, or be distrustful of those whose assistance they could use."

In a study of the highly creative design firm IDEO, the academics mapped the firm's "networks of help" and found that they were widespread and dense. In addition, "status is no barrier to being asked for help at IDEO. Low-level people are willing to approach those at the top—who, conversely, are not afraid to make themselves vulnerable by asking for help from people several levels down." By asking for help themselves, top executives signal through their outsize influence that helping and being helped is expected and encouraged.

The company makes it a point to assign outside helpers to assist project teams, and it also sets up gatherings—like all-office lunches—that increase the chances of serendipitous encounters with workers in other departments who have the potential to help.

"Help is embedded in the entire design process," from the company's brainstorming sessions, to its design reviews, to the many ways its teams solicit feedback. "In this way," Amabile and her colleagues found, the company "builds essential habits of mind."

In their study, these researchers sought to determine what made some people more helpful than others: Who were the most helpful people and why? They assumed that people with the most expertise on a given topic would be considered helpful, and this was true. But, surprisingly, it was more important that a helper be considered *trustworthy* (because people can feel vulnerable when asking for help) and *accessible* (as opposed to always being out of the office, running to meetings, and rarely answering emails).

In my own experience, I have found that encouraging people to be helpful is not usually the issue. Most people are happy to help when asked (except for some people in academia). No, organizations suffer not so much from a lack of helpfulness as a lack of help-*me*-ness.

When I first became CEO of BBDO, I came up with a great idea: to have everyone make a list of all their previous clients and the brands they had worked on, whether it was at BBDO or elsewhere. Then I arranged to have a database created that listed all of this information in an accessible way. I thought this would be a great way to give our people a head start when they were starting on a new pitch or working with a new client. I spent quite a lot of money to develop this database and launched it to enormous fanfare.

And barely anyone used it.

I came to realize that the database wasn't successful because it wasn't solving the right problem, which is that nobody thinks, or wants, to ask other people for help. When people are presented with a pitch opportunity, they feel they are being paid to attack the problem and solve it all on their own, and that asking for help is a sign of weakness.

So I scrapped the whole knowledge project, and instead just said to everybody, "The first thing you should do whenever you've got a new pitch for a new client is ask yourself this question: Who might be able to help? And I guarantee you that if you ask someone—almost anyone—either that person will be able to help you, or they can connect you with someone who can."

DO YOU HAVE TOO MANY LAYERS?

But while it's important to make sure good ideas don't stay buried in a drawer, and to encourage connections and collaboration between people, it's also important to ask yourself a related but different question: Is my organization's structure set up to quickly and effectively *evaluate* and *act* on new ideas? It's possible that institutional hierarchies—layers of decision-making set up to promote safety, compliance, and the status quo—will stop new ideas from rising to the surface without your even realizing it.

Our default setting as human beings—and certainly in business—is to look for reasons why *not* to do something. The more people who are required to approve an idea, the more likely that it will be smothered before it even has a chance to be tested.

In today's competitive business environment, the shorter you can make the distance between idea and execution, the better. That is what the CEO of Bayer, Bill Anderson, believes, and he is putting that idea to the test in a way that is downright radical for a 160-year-old company that has long operated along formal hierarchies, with top-down decision-making serving as the norm.

Anderson, who became CEO of Bayer in 2023, joined a company in crisis on multiple fronts. It was losing its patents on some of its most lucrative medicines; its pipeline for developing drugs was weak; and it was facing both a high debt load and costly litigation over one of its herbicides.

After outlining these daunting challenges in an article for *Fortune* in 2024, Anderson went on to describe another "sinister force" weighing on the company's strategic options: "Bureaucracy has put Bayer in a stranglehold. Our internal rules for employees span 1,362 pages. We have excellent people, with expertise in a range of disciplines and exceptional commitment to our success. But they are trapped in 12 levels of hierarchy, which puts unnecessary distance between our teams, our customers, and our products."[8]

He went on: "There was a time for hierarchical, command-and-control organizations—the 19th century, to be exact, when many workers were illiterate, information traveled at a snail's pace, and strict adherence to rules offered the competitive advantage of reliability."

But in the twenty-first century, people are more knowledgeable and skilled than ever before, and communication moves at lightning speed, he wrote. In those conditions, the competitive advantage goes to companies that can achieve creative breakthroughs with a minimum of red tape.

That's why Anderson decided to drastically reduce company-wide rules, management layers, and hierarchies in favor of a system he calls Dynamic Shared Ownership: "We have begun a massive effort to redesign every job and every process, with a radical focus on customers and products." Under the new system, 95 percent of decision-making will be in the hands of self-directed teams.

Some form of this is not uncommon at tech companies and start-ups, but it's just about unheard of at a 160-year-old pharmaceutical company employing tens of thousands of people.

There's no question that in business these days, fortune favors the fastest. And yet the drug development cycle has always been notoriously slow because of factors such as testing for safety and efficacy, clinical trials, and regulatory approvals. Of course those constraints must necessarily remain in place, but Anderson is betting that by allowing his teams, rather than his executives, to not only suggest but *implement* creative ideas, Bayer can vault ahead of its competitors.

It's a particularly dramatic—and egalitarian—way of bringing more creative ideas to the surface.

It's also a huge risk. But bringing a bold new creative idea into being always involves some degree of risk. In the next chapter, I'll show you how to gauge whether a big creative risk is worth taking.

10

MANAGING CREATIVE RISK

So far we've seen how organizations can create a separate structure that allows for creativity to flourish while the more exacting and predictable parts of the operation continue to run smoothly. But eventually, you're going to need to decide which creative ideas you should actually commit to—with precious and limited resources. It's a scary part of the process. But there are ways to make it more manageable.

Let me tell you about someone who knows how to manage creative risk with exceptional astuteness. There's a lot that business leaders can learn from her—so much so that I decided to make her the centerpiece of a speech I gave recently.

Before flying into Australia in 2024 to visit our offices there, I got a request from the head of our Sydney agency to do a twenty-minute presentation on the future of the advertising industry. Of course I agreed, but on the plane I couldn't help thinking, "This is probably going to be extremely boring. What can I do to make it more interesting?"

So when I stood up at lunchtime and saw all those people waiting expectantly for my supposed wisdom to spew forth, I said, "I think I've come up with the one question we need to ask ourselves every day as we work for our clients. And the question is: WWTD?"

Most people were scratching their heads and waiting for the answer. But one person shouted out, "What Would Taylor Do!" (I was both happy that someone had guessed the answer and also disappointed because she had stolen my next line.)

Just a few weeks before, Taylor Swift had concluded a fabulously successful series of concerts in Australia as part of her record-breaking, worldwide Eras Tour. The previous year, I had gone with my daughter and her friend to see Taylor perform at MetLife Stadium in New Jersey. My experience of that show, along with all the things I had read about her remarkable career, led me to realize how much organizations could learn from her as they seek to achieve a Creative Shift.

Taylor reinforces the fact that it's just not enough to have an incredibly creative idea. And it's also not enough to be able to perform at an outstanding level. If you really want to achieve a creative breakthrough that has a lasting impact, you must understand how to handle creative *risk*.

Managing creativity successfully within an organization depends on the ability to quantify which creative swings are worth the risk. As unpredictable as creative ideas can seem, it can be done. Taylor, for one, has done it.

Taylor and her team understand both the power of fame and its inherent risks, and she does everything possible to build on the power and mitigate those risks. Here's how:

She's always thinking about her next move. I remember taking my son to a Rolling Stones concert and he said, "Wow, the Rolling Stones are the world's best Rolling Stones cover band, aren't they?" It's true. All the Stones do is carry on playing the same old songs from their early years.

Taylor isn't like that (at least so far). That's why the name of her tour was so apt: It was a review of all the distinct eras of her career, which are much more firmly delineated than is the case for most performers.

She is constantly looking for ways to reinvent herself, and the shifts that she makes are significant. There's been country Taylor, pop Taylor, rock Taylor, indie Taylor, and folk Taylor, plus the carefully planned visual and narrative cues (and Easter eggs) that accompany these shifts.

As her frequent genre shifts attest, Taylor is not afraid to experiment. And she never rests on her laurels. She starts planning her next Creative Shift during the peak of the current era. (Business leaders, take note.)

It amazed me that while she was in the midst of the Eras Tour—where each performance was three and a half hours long—she found a way to write and record thirty-one songs for a surprise double album that dropped in April 2024. Not only that, but she and her team also arranged all the videos and social media content to go along with the launch. (Plus she traveled, sometimes across the world, to support her football-playing boyfriend all the way to the Super Bowl.)

Obviously, I don't know everything that goes on inside the Taylor Swift "lab." But based on the results, I know she must have lots and lots of ideas, and that she is smart enough to catch the good ones and make the best of them.

She sees the big play that no one else has seen, and she turns problems into opportunities. When the talent manager and record executive Scooter Braun bought the master recordings to Taylor's first six albums, effectively shutting her out from any future profits from them, Taylor felt devastated and helpless. Then, acting on a suggestion from fellow performer Kelly Clarkson, she went ahead and rerecorded every single song from those albums and released them as "Taylor's Version."

It was a very creative solution to a problem that might otherwise have been resolved only after a lengthy legal battle. At the same time, it required a huge executional commitment on her part. But the massive effort paid off, and the rerecorded albums reaped significantly more sales than the originals.

Another example: Rather than working with Hollywood movie studios to release the movie of her Eras Tour, she cut a deal directly with AMC movie theaters.[1] According to the Puck news site, her father came up with that idea by asking one of those questions that's so obvious, it doesn't even occur to most people: Why does there have to be a middleman here?

Of course, she benefited financially from cutting out the middleman, and she was also able to arrange for the film to be released *while* her tour was happening, rather than waiting until a 2025 release, which the studios would have pushed for. *Taylor: The Eras Tour* (with tickets going for $19.89, the title of one of her most popular albums) quickly became the highest-grossing concert movie of all time.

How did she get AMC to agree? By giving them an opportunity to solve a major problem: Not enough people were returning to movie theaters after the pandemic.

"I can get people to come back," she said, in effect. "But these are my terms."

She and her team create magic through hard work and meticulous planning. Before her Eras Tour, Taylor engaged in six months of rigorous training, including cardio and strength conditioning, plus daily sessions on the treadmill, where she sang and re-sang all of the songs on her upcoming tour's set list. She also had three months of dance training (she readily concedes that choreographed dancing is not her strong suit). "I wanted to be so over rehearsed that I could be silly with the fans, and not lose my train of thought," she told *Time*, which named her Person of the Year for 2023.[2]

At any particular moment, maybe she's being spontaneous and maybe she's not. But just as David Blaine is able to levitate four inches off the floor effortlessly (as he did one day at the BBDO offices), she is able to pull those moments off only because of her meticulous and strenuous preparation.

She anticipates every angle. When you watch Taylor in concert, you can tell that she is aware of every single camera that is trained on her and how those camera angles will appear to the audience. And with the help of multiple, carefully placed video screens at her shows, no one feels they have a bad seat. Nobody will have a restricted view, and everybody will walk away saying it was an amazing experience, even if they were in row 365. Because wherever you sit, you'll have a stunning visual experience. And if you look at any one of the big screens, you're going to see her looking straight at you, because she's always looking at the camera.

I've seen U2 and Coldplay in concert, and they've done pretty spectacular things, but nobody's ever done it as well as Taylor has. And she has found a way to work similar kinds of magic on all the major social media platforms. The detail she puts into execution is remarkable.

She makes headlines through her generosity. By late 2024, Taylor had given a total of $197 million in bonuses to various people who worked on the Eras Tour.[3] That included the tour's truck drivers, each of whom received a handwritten note of thanks from her along with a check for $100,000. I'm sure she was genuinely grateful to all her workers, but the way she showed it was almost guaranteed to generate good press. She also donates headline-grabbing amounts to causes she supports, such as food banks, natural disaster relief, and organizations for survivors of sexual assault. One example, from *People* magazine, during the Eras Tour: "Taylor Swift Donation Helps U.K. Food Banks Serve 10,000+ Meals: 'The Most Incredible Gift.'"[4] And this is a different kind of generosity but also powerful: At music awards shows, you almost always see her getting up and dancing along to other artists' songs—and singing along, too, because she's memorized the words. And she makes a point of inviting other artists to collaborate with her.

All that generosity generates an incalculable amount of publicity and goodwill that in turn provide her with support and creative ideas when she makes her next shift.

She listens and responds to feedback from her fans. Not only is this another sign of her generosity, but it also provides crucial intelligence as she prepares to transition to a new era. One example: When she rerecorded her albums, she let her fans guide her on which songs should be singles and videos this time around.

She also acknowledges criticisms and course-corrects when necessary. For example, when fans said the video of her song "Wildest Dreams," set in Africa, played to stereotypes about Africa, she apologized and donated money from the video to an organization that supports the conservation of African parks and fights to eradicate poaching.

ALWAYS REINVENT

So how can you take a page from Taylor Swift? First, by embracing the need for regular reinvention. And by recognizing that this may not come naturally to you as a business leader.

After all, you got where you are because of the successful things you did in the past. Why take the risk of interrupting that? Because if you continue with the status quo, then you risk presiding over a long, slow decline.

To be clear, all great ideas sound great—in retrospect. Once you know something works, you get on much better terms with it. Recently Apple retired its iPod digital music player. The iPod crammed a slew of breakthroughs into a slim, elegant package. Today, Apple can look back on 450-plus million iPods sold with pride and satisfaction. But that's now. Two decades ago, Apple designers and engineers were squeezed into a room filled with chips, wires, plastic cases, and one irascible idea guy: Steve Jobs. As we all know, Jobs loved to add "one more thing."

The pressure was on. No one knew whether they had the next iMac . . . or the next Newton personal digital assistant, which had been one of Apple's flops. Imagine how it felt each time Jobs pushed for something different, something extra, something unexpected. Certainly, the team resented some of those contributions, even if they knew better than to show that resentment.

"Can we just finish this already?" they would think (to themselves). The real reason for the iPod's success is that Jobs never stopped pushing. As we say at BBDO, "If you think you're through, you probably will be."

Unlike Jobs, many leaders don't understand how to balance the Creative Shift. Too many companies stumble onto the game-winning play and then punt. PARC gave Xerox the laser printer, the mouse, and the graphical user interface. Leaders decided these ideas were too risky to pursue when copiers made so much money. So Jobs and Bill Gates cheerfully walked away with those hard-earned inspirations and built what became two of the most valuable companies on the planet.

THINK LIKE A BANKER

The vast majority of humans—including business leaders—prefer the comfort of certainty, so their tendency is to reinforce the current order of things and to shy away from risks.

In my memory, one corporate leader stands out as an exception. Ironically, he wasn't the head of a hip New York record label or the founder of a Silicon Valley start-up, but a dour banker.

Years ago, the National Australia Bank hired our Australian agency to create an advertising campaign. The problem was this: NAB had introduced several consumer-friendly products and service improvements, but Australian customers harbored a deep-seated belief that the country's four big banks were in cahoots with each other, and they couldn't get past this to listen to stories about products and services. To shake up that entrenched perception, we developed a campaign where NAB "broke up" with its fellow banks on Valentine's Day. The cheeky campaign won multiple industry awards, including the Grand Prix for effectiveness at Cannes.

Remember: Before the idea worked, it looked very different. To NAB's leaders, even nodding at big bank collusion in an ad seemed wildly risky. At least, that's what I assumed.

"That was a bold thing you did," I told NAB chief executive Ross McEwan. He replied, "You're out of your mind. I'm a banker. I'm not paid to be bold. I'm paid to manage risk. When your people showed me that idea, I calculated the downside and figured while we might be laughed at or pilloried in the press or on late-night TV for a few weeks, we wouldn't lose a corporate client or a retail customer. At worst, I'd face a few awkward moments at the golf club. On the basis that I could live with the downside, I went ahead."

When you're considering a big new idea, ask yourself these questions: What is the worst thing that can happen? And can I live with that or not?

I recommend setting up a creative risk matrix with four quadrants, two at the top and two at the bottom. On the top, try to specify what the best outcome would be if you didn't take the risk on the left side and what the best outcome would be if you did take the risk on the right side. And in the bottom two quadrants, describe what the worst outcome would be if you didn't take the risk on the left side and what the worst outcome would be if you did take the risk on the right.

Of course, you can't know with absolute certainty what the best and worst outcomes will be. But the bottom line is this: If you're reasonably sure you can live with the downside, and the upside looks reasonably promising, then you can live with the uncertainty of the risk. That gives you the license to do things you wouldn't ordinarily do. Quantify the downside and make the call. Therefore, to lead a more creative organization, think like a banker.

NEW IDEAS NEED RESOURCES

And showing a commitment to creativity can't just be all talk. "You have to build in financial resources for the big swing," said Jeff Immelt, the former chief executive of GE, in a recent interview.[5] "The best leaders do that."

At legacy companies, "many things fail because they're just not funded," he said. They're considered hobbies, and they're not taken seriously. "But the worst thing you can do is say, 'Hey, we want everybody to be creative this month' and then not give them any resources to do it."

Jeff was the head of GE's health-care business in the 1990s. "In those days all the X-rays were film based. I had a unique design to do the first digital-based X-ray system, and it took $45 million to do it," he noted.

"So I went to my boss at that time and said, 'I'd love to have $45 million to invest in a digital X-ray because this is the way the world is going and we want to be the first.'" His boss said yes, that sounded like a great idea and Jeff should give it a try. But, unfortunately, his boss wouldn't be able to give him any money for it.

Jeff recalled, "So I went to our supplier, to the guy who built our digital panels, and I said, you pay for the panels, and then I'll pay you 30 percent more for the panels for the next five years and that's how you'll get your money back." The supplier agreed.

"So then I became CEO and I'm doing a review of the health-care business and people are saying we've got great products but our margins suck because some idiot signed this contract with our panel supplier," Jeff said. "And I said, 'I know that idiot quite well.'"

But he doesn't regret the decision, because that *was* the way the world was going, and the machines were a success. "There are a thousand reasons not to do something," he said. "This is what it took to get it done." And after the sixth year he no longer had to pay extra for the panels.

Jeff resolved not to be like his former boss when he started encouraging his people to participate in the Imagination Breakthroughs that were part of the company's transition from buying and selling things to inventing new products and processes. It was a major shift.

At one time, Jeff thought that if he ever wrote a book, he would call it *$2 Million from Greatness*.

Actually, when he did end up writing a book, it was called *Hot Seat*, a reflection of what it felt like to lead a company in crisis and at a crossroads after it had thrived under someone who had become a legend (Jack Welch).

"I can't tell you how many GE leaders give me the excuse 'I could fund new innovations but I can't afford it. I can't fit it into my budget,'" Jeff wrote in *Hot Seat*.[6] But that's not true. "These are from leaders that have a billion-dollar base-cost budget! Investors expect companies to take risks."

With Imagination Breakthroughs, "the idea was to cultivate ideas that were not quite ready for prime time," he wrote, "to give them not just funding but also a little protection. I knew that in a large company, ideas were particularly vulnerable when in a nascent stage."

At an operationally focused company like GE, it was important to create a separate lane for experimentation and testing, and to give people permission to fail. Obviously, you're going to need to test something quite a lot if your idea is to use, say, a new 3D material on a jet engine. Measurements to track progress were required, and in an operationally focused culture like GE's, people responded well to them.

"When people came in to champion their proposals, I told them I didn't want long-winded PowerPoint presentations," he wrote. "I wanted a short summary and a willingness to answer my questions. I usually started with three: What is the biggest internal barrier you face? What is the biggest external barrier you face? What is the revenue flow?" Within a year, GE had approved eighty Imagination Breakthroughs, and two years later twenty-five of those were generating revenue.

Jeff would review the various projects on a regular basis to see how they were performing, then decide which ones to continue. If the metrics after a year or so showed a project wasn't worth pursuing, then it would be discontinued, without negative repercussions for the people involved as long as they had shown commitment to the effort. And throughout, it was critical to be transparent about the status of each project.

"The best way to get results is to have open and honest dialogues about how you're actually doing, and that's all part of GE's problem-solving culture," Jeff said in the interview.

Fast, honest feedback is one of the greatest gifts to creative thinking. A quick "no" beats a slow "maybe" every time. You can always come up with more ideas, but there's only so much you can do to finesse one that isn't right. Leaders must give that direct feedback, make it about the idea, not the person, and get people back to work.

Paul Michaels, former president of Mars Inc. and one of my all-time favorite clients, was an absolute genius at this. He took a stand for creativity inside a company that had previously had a very conservative way of approaching new ideas.

Paul delivered very quick feedback with the help of something he had invented called the Excite-O-Meter, a half circle with a dial and a movable arrow. The dial featured ten slices of categories that ranged from "WOW!!" to "HOT STUFF" to "IT'S GOT POTENTIAL," then "OK I GUESS," "YOU'RE KIDDING ME," and "OVER YOUR DEAD BODY."

The Excite-O-Meter was a very effective EKG for ideas. Putting that dial between the idea maker and the idea—and injecting some humor into the proceedings—took some of the pressure off and made the whole process more about judging the idea itself than about judging the person behind it. It made you forget that there was a power differential and moved you into a separate creative space.

Now, Paul was a very smart guy and he was almost always right in his judgments. So when he decided to go ahead with an idea, even if it seemed pretty risky, you could be reasonably sure he was making the right call.

WHAT COULD GO WRONG?

I felt that way about David Abbott when he led AMV BBDO: that he could do no wrong. So whenever he said an idea was bad, good, or great, we took it as gospel. And that was almost always the case. Except for that one time when it was spectacularly *not* the case.

I mean, this was David Abbott working with John Cleese on a commercial. Nothing could possibly go wrong. Could it? It certainly didn't the first time these two creative geniuses teamed up to do a commercial for Sainsbury's.

The first commercial, released during the holiday season, had Cleese wearing a festive apron and standing at a table packed with holiday delicacies. Sweeping all the cooking utensils off the table with one clattery movement, he proceeded to show how easy it was to pass off Sainsbury's food as homemade.

Leaning in conspiratorially toward the viewer and flashing that wide-eyed, mock-innocent look he does so well, he said, "You see the secret is, get someone else to do the work."

The "Sainsbury's: Everybody's Favourite Ingredient" campaign was a success, so it was a no-brainer to bring Abbott and Cleese together for another commercial a few years later. This one was meant to reposition the brand to focus on its low prices, because many people perceived Sainsbury's as good quality but expensive. (We had invented the line, "Good food costs less at Sainsbury's," but all people heard was "Good food.")

I remember us going in with the account director and showing the first cut of the finished film to Sainsbury's head of marketing. When it was finished, he reacted with deathly silence. Then he said one word—"Okay"—in a grim monotone, and that was it. It was too late in the process to go back. We had to run the ad.

The television ad consists of Cleese wearing a loud suit and walking stiffly along a Sainsbury's aisle while shouting at the top of his lungs just about the whole time about what a good value Sainsbury's is. If it was supposed to be some kind of modified version of a Monty Python sketch, it failed miserably. (You can look up the "Value to Shout About" ad on YouTube if you happen to crave an ear-grating experience.)

The commercial was so universally reviled that *Marketing* magazine voted it the most irritating advert of the year for 1998. In an article headlined, "Something to Keep Quiet About," *The Guardian* reported that the campaign had been "nothing to shout about at all," and that at Sainsbury's, it had "backfired, leaving sales down and profit margins depressed."[7]

Cleese fled the country and sequestered himself in an apartment in Germany until the vitriol blew over.

Fortunately, one of the tenets of BBDO's culture is that we get up quickly after being knocked down. This was an especially powerful KO punch, but we were determined to recover from it.

Not unreasonably, we were fired from the Sainsbury's account after the "Value to Shout About" disaster—except for the black-and-white print advertising. Some people said we should drop that as well, but I thought we should hang on to it so we could stay in contact with the company and hopefully win the rest of the business back one day.

And because our people were still walking the corridors at Sainsbury's, we learned that the new agency was having trouble with the account as well. So Peter Souter, then the executive creative director of Abbott Mead Vickers BBDO in London, came up with an idea for a campaign that featured the chef Jamie Oliver, whose cooking show on the BBC was just taking off. We figured he was a brilliant representation of good food that wasn't too fussy, and that recipes by Oliver featuring Sainsbury's ingredients would be a hit with consumers.

We presented the idea to Sainsbury's new head of marketing on a Thursday, and she said, "If you can get Jamie Oliver to sign a contract by Tuesday morning, I'll give you the business back." Did I mention that this was the Thursday before Easter?

At the time, Jamie was almost more interested in Scarlet Division, the band he played drums for, than he was in cooking, and he was holed up in a garage somewhere rehearsing. In this mostly pre-cellphone age we weren't able to reach him. A colleague and I spent Saturday and Sunday of Easter weekend calling each other every thirty minutes and saying, "Have you heard anything?"

We finally tracked Jamie down that Monday and convinced him to sign a letter of intent, and on the strength of that we got the business back.

Since the release of "Value to Shout About," I've often asked myself why we let such a terrible ad see the light of day. And the honest answer is this: Because David Abbott had never been wrong before, and John Cleese was one of the most popular comedians in Britain. We let our awe of them drown out the intuitive voice inside telling us it was a terrible idea. And we spent a lot of money on something that should have been killed in the idea-generation stage.

FEEDBACK, GOOD AND BAD

When we pitched the "Good Things Come to Those Who Wait" campaign to Guinness in the late 1990s, we showed them a poster of a man sitting on a beach with a surfboard, waiting for the perfect wave. Andy Fennell, who was brand manager of Guinness at the time (he went on to become chief marketing officer for Diageo), said, "You know, you could turn that into a good television commercial," and we subsequently took his advice.

The black-and-white commercial, directed by Jonathan Glazer and filmed in Hawaii, starts out with a long close-up of a surfer's face as he waits for the right wave. An urgent electronic beat comes to a crescendo as a group of surfers charges into the water. The "white horses" of the waves turn into an actual herd of white horses who ride the ocean along with the surfers. The surfer in the close-up is the one who vanquishes the wave, and he and his buddies celebrate on the shore.

"Here's to waiting," says the stern announcer, and then a pint of Guinness appears on the screen, along with the line, "Good things come to those who . . ."

The commercial was fantastically over budget, and as it was going into production I looked at the storyboard and said to the creative team, Tom Carty and Walter Campbell, "Do you think we could do without the horses?" They looked at me as if I was mad, and thankfully they ignored me. This ad has been proclaimed by many to be the greatest commercial of all time, but it wouldn't have been if the people who created it had listened to my boneheaded feedback at the time. (Look up "Guinness-Surfer" on YouTube to understand just how much that ad would have lost without the horses.)

Feedback that runs in one direction only—from the top to the bottom—can work (most of the time) if a truly brilliant and visionary person is at the top making the decisions.

But creativity in most organizations can, and should, flow in the other direction, too. Most CEOs have no problem shutting down other people's ideas when they become aggravating (and good ideas are almost always aggravating). I've seen it happen too many times to count. As a leader, it's your responsibility to fight that urge.

Jeff Immelt said he liked to throw out "half an idea" to someone else and have them run with it. It's something he did with BBDO when he asked us for help in coming up with the "Imagination at Work" effort. And he did it with his people at GE, too.

"Truth be told, sometimes 'half an idea' was an exaggeration—what I was thinking was a quarter baked at best," he wrote in *Hot Seat*.[8] "But getting fresh eyes on something I'd been noodling over helped me in three ways: it gave me valued feedback on whether the idea was worth more of our time; it told my people that I trusted them; and it usually resulted in something better than what I'd given them in the first place."

One thing I noticed when working with Jeff was that he always asked lots and lots of questions at meetings. This was a deliberate and highly effective strategy on his part. Sometimes he did it to lead people to a conclusion he already had in mind; other times he did it to obtain valuable feedback. He told me it was a way to indicate that he, as the CEO of GE, didn't think he had all the answers, and that no single other person in the room had all the answers, either.

When managing creative risk, it's generally much better to construct a *feedback loop* that takes opinions from multiple angles into account than to rely on just one person's judgment. This is something that GE also did: It set up a group of people with diverse backgrounds and expertise—people from within the company and from outside—to weigh in on new proposals. Not during the idea-generation stage, though. Afterward.

Feedback groups need to be carefully selected and managed. Naysaying is a necessary part of the process, but it can quickly go too far. If you run an idea by too many people, or the wrong people, they can all find a different reason to say no to it before it even has a chance to breathe. Hearing all these noes, leaders can become so focused on all the imperfections of an idea that they're afraid to move forward until all aspects of it are absolutely perfect—which means never. It's true: Perfect is the enemy of good.

In his book *The Lean Startup*, the serial entrepreneur Eric Ries shows how feedback loops can be used efficiently to help manage creative risk. He emphasizes that his approach can be utilized in a variety of organizations, both large and small.

"I've come to believe that learning is the essential unit of progress," Ries writes.[9] He believes in the power of "validated learning," which shows up in the form of quantifiable data. "It's easy to kid yourself about what customers want. It's also easy to learn things that are completely irrelevant. Thus, validated learning is backed up by empirical data collected from real customers."

How do you learn what your customers really want without wasting time and money? By developing what Ries calls a "Build-Measure-Learn" feedback loop.[10] It starts with "a leap-of-faith hypothesis" and then moves to testing that hypothesis on a small scale by building a "minimum viable product." The MVP will be primitive and imperfect, but if it is designed correctly, you can measure the results and learn valuable information that can tell you whether to persevere with your idea or not.

He gives Zappos as an example of a company that did this.[11] In the late 1990s the founder, Nick Swinmurn, had a hypothesis: that customers would be willing to buy shoes over the internet. But he had no way of knowing if that was actually true.

"Swinmurn could have waited a long time, insisting on testing his complete vision completely with warehouses, distribution partners, and the promise of significant sales," Ries writes. "Many early e-commerce pioneers did just that, including infamous dot-com failures such as Webvan and Pets.com."

Instead, Swinmurn "began by asking local shoe stores if he could take pictures of their inventory. In exchange for permission to take the pictures, he would post the pictures online," he explained, as a product for sale on his own site. Then he would "come back to buy the shoes at full price if a customer bought them online."

Based on this bare-bones experiment, Swinmurn gained a lot of information. He learned from his customers' feedback, for example, that they *were* willing to buy shoes online. After analyzing sales and customer behavior, he refined his business model further, did more experiments, and scaled up from there.

Zappos, of course, was a resounding success. And in 2009, Amazon bought the company for more than $1 billion.

In many other cases, the minimum viable product will produce results showing that the leap-of-faith hypothesis was based on flawed assumptions. Imagine a different scenario, where customers did not respond in ways that would lead to a sustainable business model. In which case, good! You've learned something, and now it's time to try a different experiment. Failure is a necessary part of the process.

Or, what if you conducted an experiment that yielded results that were surprising? Also good! That could cause you to pivot toward a new use for your product or service.

Just look at Thomas Edison, the founder of GE. Sure, he's known for the light bulb, the phonograph, the movie camera, and many other inventions. But he also came up with a talking doll; an ore miller and separator; a tinfoil phonograph; a home projector kinetoscope; and other inventions that were poorly designed and/or that never found success in the marketplace (although they did often inspire other inventors to come up with their own versions, or inspire him to think of creative alternatives). A willingness to do lots of experiments, and to persevere and to change direction when necessary, were key to Edison's success.

In his best-selling book *Where Good Ideas Come From*, Steven Johnson, the innovation expert, quotes the British economist William Stanley Jevons as saying, "The errors of the great mind exceed in number those of the less vigorous one."[12] Johnson adds that studies of patent records have shown that overall productivity (presumably including plenty of work with errors) "correlates with radical breakthroughs in science and technology."

Once again, it comes down to this: You're going to be wrong—a lot—before you come up with the right ideas and the right application of those ideas. What can be hard to accept is that bad ideas and failure are inherent to the Creative Shift. And because they are, you need to be as efficient as possible about including them in the process, rather than trying to pretend that you don't need them at all or can avoid them entirely.

It's uncomfortable. It's uncertain. It's also the only way to grow and evolve, especially in today's unpredictable world.

So keep the ideas coming from all over and give the long shots a chance. Once you've identified and quantified the downside—it's usually not as bad as you fear—it's time to set up your next Creative Shift.

That's what Taylor would do.

ACKNOWLEDGMENTS

I'm going to imagine that I'm at the Academy Awards and that some music will cut me off if I go on too long.

I soaked with the idea for this book for a while and wasn't sure it needed to be written, so I'd like to thank Sandy Lutton, and Lori Lee, who both responded the same way when I told them about it: "You should totally write that book." I am also indebted to Peter Sherman and my son, Angus, who were kind enough to read the first draft, generous enough to tell me to keep going with it, and honest enough to tell me how I could improve it.

Phyllis Korkki was a patient, resourceful, and disciplined collaborator. Colleen Lawrie gave me the gift of saying, "I'm having lunch with my editor," something I had always longed to do, and along with Roger Labrie edited with a light but firm hand. Thanks also to Executive Editor Emily Taber and to Lynn Johnston, my agent.

But the experience that really mattered was mine at BBDO—especially the truly brilliant creative people I worked with around the world and the amazing clients who took me into their confidence. Many are quoted or mentioned in this book. Many more of them are not.

And for the opportunity to have those experiences I thank John Wren, chairman and CEO of Omnicom Inc., who appointed me as president and CEO, thrust me into the limelight when things went well, and shielded me from the searchlight when they didn't.

Finally, my deepest gratitude goes to my wife, Sue; my daughters, Amy and Louisa; and my son, Angus, for the encouragement and support they have always given me and the humorous way they've pierced my balloon when I needed it.

(Music starts.)

NOTES

INTRODUCTION

1. "Case Study: InterQ Partnered with Delta Air Lines to Decrease Passenger Stress While Flying," InterQ, accessed December 10, 2024, https://interq-research.com/case-study-interq-partnered-with-delta-airlines-to-decrease-passenger-stress-while-flying.

CHAPTER ONE: WHY THE CREATIVITY SHIFT WORKS

1. Julien Boudet, Biljana Cvetanovski, Brian Gregg, Jason Heller, and Jesko Perry, "The Marketing Recipe for Growth: Creativity, Data, and Relationships," McKinsey, July 2, 2019, www.mckinsey.com/capabilities/growth-markeating-and-sales/our-insights/the-marketing-recipe-for-growth-creativity-data-and-relationships.
2. "Known and Unknown: Author's Note," Rumsfeld Papers, December 2010, https://papers.rumsfeld.com/about/page/authors-note (emphasis added).
3. FedEx fact sheet.
4. Keith McNally (keithmcnallynyc), Instagram, December 16, 2023, www.instagram.com/keithmcnallynyc/p/C0744yUMScx.
5. Will Guidara, *Unreasonable Hospitality: The Remarkable Power of Giving People More Than They Expect* (New York: Optimism Press, 2022), chap. 5.
6. Guidara, *Unreasonable Hospitality*, chap. 18.
7. Video interview, February 6, 2024.

8. Protectstar Inc., "iPhone 1: Steve Jobs MacWorld Keynote in 2007—Full Presentation, 80 mins," 2007, YouTube, posted May 16, 2013, www.youtube.com/watch?v=VQKMoT-6XSg.

9. Robert L. Leahy, "Are You a CrackBerry? How to Break Free from Addictive Checking," *Psychology Today*, April 21, 2010, www.psychologytoday.com/intl/blog/anxiety-files/201004/are-you-a-crackberry-how-to-break-free-from-addictive-checking.

10. *BlackBerry*, directed by Matt Johnson, IFC Films, 2023.

11. Sam Gustin, "The Fatal Mistake That Doomed BlackBerry," *Time*, September 24, 2013, https://business.time.com/2013/09/24/the-fatal-mistake-that-doomed-blackberry.

12. Ranjay Gulati and Nicole Tempest Keller, "Transforming BlackBerry: From Smartphones to Software," Harvard Business School Case 421-052, April 2021.

13. Jeff Immelt, *Hot Seat: What I Learned Leading a Great American Company* (New York: Avid Reader Press / Simon and Schuster, 2021), chap. 1.

14. Video interview, March 26, 2024.

15. Video interview, February 27, 2024.

CHAPTER TWO: THE WORKOUT

1. Adam Grant, "Why Brainstorming Doesn't Work," *Time*, October 24, 2023, https://time.com/6327515/brainstorming-doesnt-work-essay.

2. Alex Faickney Osborn, *Applied Imagination: Principles and Procedures of Creative Thinking* (New York: Scribner, 1953).

3. California College of the Arts—CCA, "Sir Jony Ive's 2021 CCA Commencement Honorary Doctorate Address," May 10, 2021, YouTube, posted May 13, 2021, www.youtube.com/watch?v=gr3GKcwG9s8.

4. Tina Fey, *Bossypants* (New York: Little Brown, 2011), chap. 8.

5. Teresa Amabile, Constance N. Hadley, and Steven J. Kramer, "Creativity Under the Gun," *Harvard Business Review* 80, no. 8 (August 2002).

6. Video interviews, February 15 and 23, 2024.

7. Video interview, April 23, 2024.

NOTES

CHAPTER THREE: THE CULTURE OF THE CREATIVE SHIFT

1. Will Guidara, *Unreasonable Hospitality: The Remarkable Power of Giving People More Than They Expect* (New York: Optimism Press, 2022), chap. 4.

2. Liz Wiseman, *Multipliers: How the Best Leaders Make Everyone Smarter*, rev. ed. (New York: HarperCollins, 2017), chap. 1.

3. Wiseman, *Multipliers*, preface.

4. Wiseman, *Multipliers*, chap. 1.

5. Video interview, April 10, 2024.

6. Beth Comstock, with Tahl Raz, *Imagine It Forward: Courage, Creativity, and the Power of Change* (New York: Crown Currency, 2018), chap. 2.

7. Comstock, *Imagine It Forward*, chap. 4.

8. Video interview, March 26, 2024.

9. Video interview, July 29, 2024.

10. Quotations from Amy Edmondson here and below are from her interview with Karen Christensen, "The Fearless Organization," *Rotman Management Magazine*, May 1, 2019.

11. Walter Isaacson, *Elon Musk* (New York: Simon and Schuster, 2023), chap. 81.

12. Isaacson, *Elon Musk*, chap. 67.

13. Isaacson, *Elon Musk*, chap. 59.

14. Isaacson, *Elon Musk*, chap. 25.

15. Isaacson, *Elon Musk*, chap. 88.

16. Tina Fey, *Bossypants* (New York: Little Brown, 2011), chap. 13.

17. Wiseman, *Multipliers*.

18. Video interview, February 6, 2024.

19. Milan Vego, "On Military Creativity," *Joint Force Quarterly*, no. 70 (Third Quarter 2013).

20. Angus Fletcher, *Creative Thinking: A Field Guide to Building Your Strategic Core* (independently published, 2021).

21. Chris Bournea, "Ohio State Professor Angus Fletcher Awarded U.S. Army Medal for Leadership Training," Ohio State News Service, March 7, 2023, https://news.osu.edu/ohio-state-professor-angus-fletcher-awarded-us-army-medal-for-leadership-training.

22. Video interview, April 9, 2024.

23. Sarah Mervosh, "Who Runs the Best U.S. Schools? It May Be the Defense Department," *New York Times*, October 10, 2023, www.nytimes.com/2023/10/10/us/schools-pandemic-defense-department.html.

CHAPTER FOUR: DO IT THE WRONG WAY FIRST. A LOT.

1. Video interview, January 25, 2024.

2. Video interview, April 9, 2024.

3. D&AD, ed., *The Copy Book: How Some of the Best Advertising Writers in the World Write Their Advertising* (Los Angeles: Taschen America, 2018), chap. 1.

4. Startup Archive, "Steve Jobs Explains the Difference Between a Great Idea and a Great Product," YouTube, posted January 14, 2024, https://youtube.com/watch?v=sm1msysj5lw.

CHAPTER FIVE: HARNESS THE CREATIVE POWER OF YOUR PEOPLE

1. Video interviews, February 6 and April 1, 2024.

2. John Cleese, "Creativity in Management," speech delivered to Video Arts, 1991, transcript at James Clear website, https://jamesclear.com/great-speeches/creativity-in-management-by-john-cleese.

3. Donald W. MacKinnon, "Identification and Development of Creativity Abilities," University of California, Berkeley, Institute of Personality Assessment and Research, March 14, 1964, available at Institute of Education Sciences (ERIC), US Department of Education, https://files.eric.ed.gov/fulltext/ED027965.pdf.

4. Johan Roos and Bart Victor, "How It All Began: The Origins of LEGO Serious Play," *International Journal of Management and Applied Research* 5, no. 4 (2018): 326–343.

5. "LEGO Serious Play Methodology: What Is It Exactly?," LEGO USA Serious Play Facilitators, accessed February 2, 2025, https://seriousplay.community/usa/methodology.

6. Mads Bab and Ilona Boniwell, *Exploring Positive Psychology with LEGO Serious Play: A Hands On Thinking Guide* (Aarhus, Denmark: Gnist, 2016).

7. Land summarizes his findings described here at TEDx Talks, "TedxTucson, George Land, the Failure of Success," YouTube, February 16, 2011, www.youtube.com/watch?v=ZfKMq-rYtnc.

8. Alison Gopnik, Shaun O'Grady, Christopher G. Lucas, and Ronald E. Dahl, "Changes in Cognitive Flexibility and Hypothesis Search Across Human Life History from Childhood to Adolescence to Adulthood," *Proceedings of the National Academy of Sciences* 114, no. 30 (2017): 7892–7899, available at PNAS, www.pnas.org/doi/10.1073/pnas.1700811114.

9. Video interview, April 9, 2024.

10. Video interview, March 14, 2024.

11. Tom Kelley and David Kelley, *Creative Confidence: Unleashing the Creative Potential Within Us All* (New York: Crown Currency, 2013), chap. 6.

12. Video interview, March 18, 2024.

13. Walter Isaacson, *Elon Musk* (New York: Simon and Schuster, 2023), chap. 17.

14. Video interviews, January 22 and March 19, 2024.

15. "Ozone Layer Recovery Is on Track, Helping Avoid Global Warming by 0.5°," press release, United Nations Environment Programme, January 9, 2023, www.unep.org/news-and-stories/press-release/ozone-layer-recovery-track-helping-avoid-global-warming-05degc.

16. Beth Comstock, with Tahl Raz, *Imagine It Forward: Courage, Creativity and the Power of Change* (New York: Crown Currency, 2018), chap 4.

CHAPTER SIX: STEP ONE OF THE SHIFT

1. "Edwin Land and Polaroid Photography," American Chemical Society, accessed December 17, 2024, www.acs.org/education/whatischemistry/landmarks/land-instant-photography.html.

2. "Understanding the '5 Whys' Methodology," StanfordH4d's Newsletter, Substack, April 30, 2024, https://stanfordh4d.substack.com/p/understanding-the-5-whys-methodology.

3. Walter Isaacson, *Elon Musk* (New York: Simon and Schuster, 2023), chap. 18.

4. Daniel J. Simons and Christopher F. Chabris, "Gorillas in Our Midst: Sustained Inattentional Blindness for Dynamic Events," *Perception* 28, no. 9 (1999): 1059–1074.

5. Morihei Ueshiba, *The Art of Peace*, trans. John Stevens (Boulder: Shambhala, 2007).

6. Jeremy Thorpe-Woods, "Guinness: Good Things Come to Those Who Wait," World Advertising Research Center (WARC), accessed February 2, 2025, www.warc.com/content/paywall/article/apg /guinness-good-things-come-to-those-who-wait/en-gb/49760.

CHAPTER SEVEN: PRIMING THE BRAIN FOR BREAKTHROUGHS

1. Steven Johnson, *Where Good Ideas Come From: The Natural History of Innovation* (New York: Riverhead Books, 2010), chap. 3.

2. "Mark Zuckerberg's Commencement Address at Harvard," *Harvard Gazette,* May 25, 2017, https://news.harvard.edu/gazette /story/2017/05/mark-zuckerbergs-speech-as-written-for-harvards -class-of-2017.

3. Steven Johnson, *Where Good Ideas Come From: The Natural History of Innovation* (New York: Riverhead Books, 2010), chap. 3.

4. "To Better Understand Your Customers, Think Like a 'Consumer Anthropologist,'" *Kellogg Insight,* April 5, 2023, https://insight .kellogg.northwestern.edu/article/to-better-understand-your -customers-think-like-a-consumer-anthropologist.

5. "Roger Federer, Lionel Messi, and the Pursuit of Greatness," *The Economist,* August 7, 2021, www.economist.com/culture/2021/08/07 /roger-federer-lionel-messi-and-the-pursuit-of-greatness.

6. Video interview, March 14, 2024.

7. "The Ritual Masters," a BBDO-commissioned study, 2007.

8. Video interview, March 14, 2024.

9. Tom Kelley and David Kelley, *Creative Confidence: Unleashing the Creative Potential Within Us All* (New York: Crown Currency, 2013), chap. 1.

10. Kelley and Kelley, *Creative Confidence,* chap. 3.

11. Mike Isaac, "Mark Zuckerberg's Great American Road Trip," *New York Times*, May 25, 2017.

12. "Mark Zuckerberg's Commencement Address at Harvard."

13. Helen Demetriou and Bill Nicholl, "Empathy Is the Mother of Invention: Emotion and Cognition for Creativity in the Classroom," *Improving Schools* 25, no. 1 (2021): 4–21, available at Sage Journals, https://journals.sagepub.com/doi/full/10.1177/13654802219 89500.

14. "'Strength in Stillness': Bob Roth Explains the Benefits of Transcendental Meditation," Women's Alzheimer's Movement, February 27, 2018, https://thewomensalzheimersmovement.org/strength-in -stillness-bob-roth.

15. Marilyn Oppezzo and Daniel L. Schwartz, "Give Your Ideas Some Legs: The Positive Effect of Walking on Creative Thinking," *Journal of Experimental Psychology: Learning, Memory, and Cognition* 40, no. 4 (2014): 1142–1152, available at American Psychological Association, www.apa.org/pubs/journals/releases/xlm-a0036577.pdf.

16. Brittany Anas, "The Rawdogging Flights Trend, Explained," *Forbes*, August 26, 2024, www.forbes.com/sites/brittanyanas/2024/08 /26/the-rawdogging-flights-trend-explained.

CHAPTER EIGHT: ACTIVATE YOUR SPACE

1. Alina Dizik, "The Benefits of Eavesdropping on Office Conversations," *The Wall Street Journal*, June 10, 2023, www.wsj.com/articles /eavesdropping-office-conversations-ae574d68.

2. "History," Gandhi Ashram at Sabarmati, accessed December 18, 2024, www.gandhiashramsabarmati.org/en/about-gandhi-ashram -menu/history-menu.html.

3. Video interview, March 14, 2024.

4. "This Was the Best of the Best in Advertising from the Past 12 Months," Business Insider India, July 26, 2021, www.businessinsider .in/advertising/this-was-the-best-of-the-best-in-advertising-from-the -past-12-months/slidelist/47865936.cms#slideid=47865938.

CHAPTER NINE: CATCHING IDEAS

1. "David Lynch on Big Ideas," Big Think, October 20, 2014, https://bigthink.com/words-of-wisdom/david-lynch-on-big-ideas.

2. David A. Hofmann and John J. Sumanth, "Get Your Employees to Make Better Suggestions," *Harvard Business Review*, March 5, 2015, https://hbr.org/2015/03/get-your-employees-to-make-better-suggestions.

3. Video interview, March 18, 2024.

4. Richard Sandomir, "Spencer Silver, an Inventor of Post-it Notes, Is Dead at 80," *New York Times*, May 13, 2021, www.nytimes.com/2021/05/13/business/spencer-silver-dead.html.

5. Nick Glass and Tim Hume, "The 'Hallelujah Moment' Behind the Invention of the Post-it Note," CNN Business, April 4, 2013, www.cnn.com/2013/04/04/tech/post-it-note-history/index.html.

6. *A Century of Innovation: The 3M Story*, 3M Company, 2002, online at 3m.com, https://multimedia.3m.com/mws/media/171240O/3m-century-of-innovation-book.pdf.

7. Teresa M. Amabile, Colin M. Fisher, and Julianna Pillemer, "IDEO's Culture of Helping," *Harvard Business Review*, January 2014.

8. Bill Anderson, "Bayer CEO: Corporate Bureaucracy Belongs in the 19th Century. Here's How We're Fighting It," *Fortune*, March 21, 2024, https://fortune.com/2024/03/21/bayer-ceo-bill-anderson-corporate-bureaucracy-19th-century-leadership.

CHAPTER TEN: MANAGING CREATIVE RISK

1. Matthew Belloni, "How the Swiftie Cinematic Universe Came to Theaters," *Puck*, September 1, 2023, https://puck.news/how-the-swiftie-cinematic-universe-came-to-theaters.

2. Sam Lansky, "Person of the Year: Taylor Swift," *Time*, December 6, 2023, https://time.com/6342806/person-of-the-year-2023-taylor-swift.

3. Melody Chiu and Jeff Nelson, "Taylor Swift Gave a Whopping $197 Million in Bonuses to Eras Tour Performers, Crew on Top of Their Salaries," *People*, December 9, 2024, https://people.com/taylor-swift-gave-eras-tour-crew-usd197-million-in-bonuses-exclusive-8758216.

4. Angel Saunders, "Taylor Swift Donation Helps U.K. Food Banks Serve 10,000+ Meals:'The Most Incredible Gift,'" *People*, June 25, 2024, https://people.com/taylor-swift-donation-helps-uk-food-banks-8669288.

5. Video interview, March 26, 2024.

6. Jeff Immelt, *Hot Seat: What I Learned Leading a Great American Company* (New York: Avid Reader Press / Simon and Schuster, 2021), chap 4.

7. Julia Finch, "Something to Keep Quiet About," *Guardian*, February 5, 1999, www.theguardian.com/business/1999/feb/06/1.

8. Immelt, *Hot Seat*.

9. Eric Ries, *The Lean Startup: How Today's Entrepreneurs Use Continuous Innovation to Create Radically Successful Businesses* (New York: Crown Currency, 2011), chap. 3.

10. Ries, *Lean Startup*, introduction.

11. Ries, *Lean Startup*, chap. 4.

12. Steven Johnson, *Where Good Ideas Come From: The Natural History of Innovation* (New York: Riverhead Books, 2010), chap. 5.

INDEX

INDEX

INDEX

INDEX

INDEX

INDEX

INDEX

INDEX

INDEX

Andrew Robertson is chairman of BBDO Worldwide. He served as president and CEO for two decades, during which BBDO was recognized in the Effie Awards Index as the world's most effective network five times and as "Network of the Decade" at the Cannes Lions Awards. Inducted into the Advertising Hall of Fame in 2022, he was named one of the one hundred most influential leaders in marketing, media, and tech alongside industry giants like Mark Zuckerberg, Tim Cook, and Jeff Bezos. He has taught guest classes at New York University, the University of North Carolina at Chapel Hill, and Wake Forest University. He has also appeared on CNBC, Bloomberg News, and *The Today Show* and is a chairman emeritus of the Advertising Council. He lives in New York City.